TRANSFORM
DENTAL SLEEP

The Step-by-Step Guide to Doubling Your Sleep Patients, Increasing Physician Referrals, Simplifying Processes, and Improving Your Life

JASON TIERNEY
Illustrated by Matthew Hodel

TRANSFORM
DENTAL SLEEP

To my muse, Lesia.
You've shown me that everything is possible.

TABLE OF CONTENTS

SECTION 1

GENESIS OF THIS BOOK

February 2019. Scottsdale, Arizona. I was sitting in another dental sleep medicine course. Pre-pandemic. But that doesn't matter. It was perhaps my 100th dental sleep medicine CE course. Or maybe the 200th.

There were 12 dentists in the meeting, plus 17 team members, 9 of whom were from one office in Wisconsin and did not hide their displeasure about having been promised a weekend of warm weather and cold drinks, not cold desert and bad food. They killed time on Facebook, joking about the food and asking who wanted to go day-drinking or windsurfing.

Doctor Dumass didn't seem particularly interested in the course's content either. He may have thought that suffering through the course would be worth it to write off a golfing and drinking trip. Do the math. Most of the dentists didn't bring any team members along to learn about a life-saving procedure, even though the workflow required delegating to the team that would make it or break it.

I was the event organizer. Given that I live in Arizona, the course was in my backyard, and so I did double duty as a sales rep for my company. That's right, I was one of *those* guys. Suit and tie amongst business casual, smiling and engaging everyone. The guy who struck fear in those considering a free bagel at 7:53 a.m.

I talked with attendees during the breaks, throwing in a few comments related to the lecture material and ensuring that the overpriced coffee carafes were at least half full. Or, depending on the group's disposition, half empty. The lecture continued, and the attendees oscillated between disinterest and questions that indicated a lack of basic understanding of the subject matter.

"What is AHI again?"

"Can't you just make them a snore appliance anyway and bill their dental insurance? This seems like a lot of work."

It was annoying, but also deplorably common. From Seattle to Tampa, I witnessed this same scenario play out dozens of times before.

After the first day of the weekend course, we always invited the attendees to join us for dinner. Most declined. However, after explaining that "be our guests" meant that we were paying, nearly everyone changed their minds. Apparently, the only thing better than sex on the beach and lukewarm linguine is FREE sex on the beach and lukewarm linguine.

At dinner, I chatted with many of the attendees about what had led them to the course. Some talked about their plans to transition out of restorative dentistry so they could focus exclusively on sleep. They asked questions that demonstrated their basic grasp of the content from the day's lecture.

Full stomachs. Lessened inhibitions. Sunshine Act be damned.

So far, so good, right? Sure, until they admitted that they had never treated a patient and had failing practices. Plus, their social awkwardness made me feel queasy. Two drunk, crying attendees later—a dentist and a hygienist—and it was time to call it a night, with Ubers on us and a reminder that we would reconvene at 8:00 a.m.

Flash forward to day two: Participants trickle in, blinded by the light (and last night's Tito's). Dr. Allan Coholic rocks Ray Bans all day while staying close to the continental breakfast table for regular coffee refills. Observing the aftermath of the previous night's drinking, the teetotalers among us were feeling the *schadenfreude* in full effect.

The lecturer was doing an exceptional job covertly weaving our product into the educational content. The morning lecture concluded, and now it was my time to shine. Time to address the group and make my sales pitch. I'd done it a zillion times, and I was certain I could summon a compelling call-to-action to purchase our product. The only thing I was more certain of was that not one of these dentists would succeed in dental sleep medicine.

I strolled to the podium and, incapable of perpetrating this fraud any longer, dismissed the group for a 20-minute break to "use the restroom, catch up on calls, or whatever you need to do."

Dr. Dan Druff hurriedly asked if he could get his CE so he could cut out a bit early. He and his assistant showed up two hours late on day one, and their uninhibited disdain for the office manager (Mrs. Druff is the office manager) was embarrassing for everyone. Dr. Druff and his "assistant" were equally vocal about their affinity for free drinks and for each other. Sure, no problem. Here's your alibi, masquerading as a CE certificate.

I knew at this point that I needed to end this phase of my career. I just couldn't do it any longer, and so I decided to put my dental sleep career to bed. Then I had a wake-up call that forced me to write this book.

GET BUSY LIVING

"It comes down to a simple choice, really. Get busy living or get busy dying."
—Andy Dufresne, The Shawshank Redemption

Joel had lived across the street from me since I moved here eight years ago. He was in his mid-fifties and retired nearly a decade earlier, after spending years in operations at a tech firm. Joel's elderly mother was suffering from dementia, and she lived with him. His days consisted of taking care of her, reading books, trail running, and tending his enviable lawn, filled with desert shrubs and gargantuan cactuses. Yes, both *cactuses* and *cacti* are acceptable plural forms of 'cactus'.

Joel and I chatted a couple times a week, usually when I was out walking my Pugs. I think it was more than just a pause from the yard work; it was an opportunity to connect and a much-needed break from the challenges of taking care of his mom. Our go-to topics included philosophy, trail running shoes, and cycling routes, but we were all over the place. These open-air chats meandered like trails through Brown's Ranch.

Occasionally he complained about his CPAP.

"It hurts my face, and it makes so much damn noise when I turn over," he complained during one of our confabs. "It wakes me up, and then I can't fall back asleep, so I just lie there until I finally just say, 'f*ck it' and get up."

Some DSM practitioners are so zealous about sleep that they'd probably run home at this point, grab a sample appliance, and give Joel a consultation right there amidst the saguaros and cholla. I'm not a proselytizer; I prefer to attract rather than dictate. I listened and then asked him what he knew about oral appliance therapy. He was oblivious to its existence.

"It's basically like a couple of retainers or nightguards that are joined together in some way, I explained. "It holds your jaw slightly forward at night to maintain an open airway. There's a ton of research out there supporting it. It doesn't always work quite as well as CPAP, but it's way more comfortable, and so patients are much more likely to actually use it."

"Yeah, I should check that out," Joel responded.

My wife co-founded several DSM practices in the Phoenix area. Later that afternoon, I left one of her business cards at Joel's front door. The next time I saw Joel, he thanked me for the card. Sensitive to being perceived as pushy, I passively floated, "No sweat. You should give them a call. A consultation won't cost you anything, and there's no obligation. It's not for everybody, but it's legit, and it's been a game-changer for a lot of people."

Late in 2021, Joel and I started making plans to run the Grand Canyon Rim-to-Rim the following May. Then, in March, Joel died in his bed. Myocardial infarction: a massive heart attack. I would bet money that his sleep apnea played a role. Joel didn't have any siblings or kids, and he'd never been married. Now he's gone, and his mother is in assisted living.

My next-door neighbor, John, had known Joel longer than I had, and he helped with the estate. A few days after Joel passed, John came over and handed me a Saucony shoe box with a brand new pair of Saucony Peregrines, size 11 ½. I also wear an 11 ½. John knew I was a trail runner and thought I might want them. During one of my discursive dialogues with Joel, I had praised these as my favorite trail running shoes and he said he'd try a pair next time. He never got the chance to use the shoes, but I wore them on the Kaibab Trail deep into the Grand Canyon and back up again.

Incidentally, John is 90-years-old, and he also has sleep apnea. He wears his CPAP every night, walks his dog three miles a day, and lifts weights a few times a week.

I'm still frustrated with the slow adoption of dental sleep medicine among the dental-medical professions, and I'm appalled by the machinations perpetrated by some insurance companies and a few commercial interests. I am absolutely certain that well-trained dentists can make a real difference if equipped with the proper motivation, the right education and tools, and a healthy dose of grit. Sleep medicine saves lives, so a mother doesn't have to lose her son and a friend doesn't have to run alone.

WHAT THIS BOOK IS
(AND ISN'T)

I've dedicated the past 20 years of my professional life to dental sleep medicine. In this time, I have studied carefully what works and what doesn't. I've sought insights from the gurus, built companies, coached practices, developed products, and helped take speakers and companies from the nadir to the pinnacle. From alpha to launch, to infinity and beyond.

During this time, well-known speakers and subject matter experts have shared with me their knowledge, wisdom, and experience. Sometimes they did so while we worked side-by-side in their offices. Other times we collaborated on articles. I've interviewed them on podcasts, and we've developed CE presentations together.

I'm also an avid reader and believer in learning analogously. What other businesses have overcome obstacles to become household names? How did they do it? What are the similarities between those obstacles and those our field faces? What can we learn from their mistakes? Their successes? Otto von Bismarck summed it up succinctly: "Only a fool learns from his own mistakes. The wise man learns from the mistakes of others." Jim Rohn takes this simple, yet powerful idea even further: "It's important to learn from your mistakes, but it is better to learn from other people's mistakes, and it is best to learn from other people's successes. It accelerates your own success."

These experiences have shown me that successful DSM practices generate a purpose and meaning for sleep in the office, resonating with the team and permeating everything they do. The plan and objectives are clearly outlined and understood by everyone. Dentists can't do it alone. It is impossible. They must delegate appropriately and empower their teams to get things done. Everyone must make relentless forward progress. It's paramount that goals and metrics be put in place so this progress can be measured, followed by appropriate actions to correct the path.

It's simple. But it's not easy.

The description above is like the instructions on the box, "Easy assembly in just five minutes." Then you open the box and pour out bags of parts, pieces, and an instruction manual in another language. Some assembly required, my @$$. Not so easy after all.

The devil is in the details, but so is salvation.

This book is not a clinical digest. It doesn't delve into which precision device you should use, nor will it tell you how to reset the arms on a Herbst or whether you need to secure a new PTAN # if you treat Medicare patients one day per week in another clinic. That information is available from myriad reliable sources. Ask me, and I'll point you to them.

My goal with this book is to strip away DSM's mystique. If you practice the principles described here, you'll create a successful DSM practice. You will also have less chaos in your life, greater career satisfaction, and happier home relationships. Guaranteed.

WHY ME?

Why am I qualified to write this book?

It's a question you might be asking yourself, and it's a fair one. I hope that by the end of this book, my words will speak for themselves, but here's a little information about me.

A few of the most widely used products and services in dental sleep have my fingerprints on them. It sounds like a boast (or a confession), and I apologize if it seems like self-aggrandizement. In some cases, I was on the periphery, sharing my opinions and insights, and in others I played principal roles in developing, launching, and promoting the products. From commonly prescribed appliances and widely used software to DSM conferences and influential articles, I've been there.

One oft-heralded KOL referred to me as "the director" because I scripted his courses and taught him how to present for maximum impact. Others have referred to me as the "hidden hand of dental sleep medicine." I'm not sure these nicknames are deserved, but they'd both look cool on a desk nameplate.

Throughout my career, I've met zillions of dentists and worked with thousands of dental practices. I've seen what works and what doesn't, noting which behavioral traits and organizational skill sets lead to high achievement and which ones lead to floundering, flailing, failing, and bailing. I've interviewed dentists and their team members, authors, DSM gurus, and key opinion leaders.

I took what I've learned and synthesized it into an easy-to-read, highly actionable book to help you communicate with your patients, team members, referring physicians, and just about everyone else in your sphere. I have nothing to sell, no lecture series, consulting package, or subscription service; I just want to help you realize your potential so your patients can realize theirs.

This book is the culmination of all those articles, interviews, books, life experiences, team meetings, leadership summits, educational events, CE sales courses, and everything else—synthesized through my brain with a sprinkling of bad jokes added for funsies.

For most of my career, I've worked behind the scenes, preferring to give credit and take responsibility. In that spirit, kudos to those whose work is referenced here and who've inspired me. These ideas and concepts are not my own; I'm not that smart. All I've done is repackage and repurpose their brilliance in dental sleep clothing.

Steven Pressfield, Marcus Aurelius, Talib Kweli, and Toby Morse. Ryan Holiday, Naval Ravikant, Robert Cialdini, and Ice-T. Barry Glassman, Jagdeep Bijwadia, Steve Carstensen, and Kent Smith. Randy Curran, The Notorious R.B.D., Jason Doucette, Lesia Tierney, Jamison Spencer, and Stacey Layman. The list goes on (and it does at the end of the book), and to each of these individuals, I am grateful. Their insights and inspiration have driven me to work to realize my potential as a human being. Inspired by their excellence, I hope to help you strive to achieve your own.

There's a much greater need for sleep medicine and more opportunities for practitioners than at any point in our history. At the same time, we still have to deal with scammers, charlatans, and cons. They have been multiplying like gremlins that were fed after midnight, and I feel an irresistible compulsion to share the truth.

This truth is presented to you in three sections. First, I'll lay out the pitfalls and obstacles dentists face in dental sleep medicine. You've likely experienced some of them. Ideally, these pages will help you avoid the others. The focus is on what hasn't worked and why it's unlikely to be any different for you.

The second section is about communication. This may seem unrelated to sleep. The most successful DSM practitioners are expert communicators. Some may be so-so clinicians, but they're able to identify what their patients and referring physicians need. They know how to help others see what a better future might look like and how they can help. You'll get tips for communicating intentionally. These will lead to more patients and physician referrals, stronger team rapport, and better relationships throughout your life.

The final section is a deep dive into the vital, yet oft-overlooked underpinnings of the top practices. I'll enumerate the steps used to achieve success and continually reach new heights. You'll see the importance of creating your "why" and how you can generate a vision that turns the entire team into ride-or-die sleep advocates. Then you'll read how to outline the path forward so that everyone is aligned and understands the "how" and the "what."

Next, we'll focus on time and resource management because you can't do it on your own. You must delegate. Analysis paralysis hinders many dentists' progress in sleep medicine. We'll overcome that when we ramp up your propensity to execute. Once you've gained some traction, what metrics should you use? What about employee reviews, hiring, and firing? You'll need to evaluate and identify what's working and what's not. Finally, what will you do with all this information? How will you make informed changes to put you on a brighter path to tomorrow?

Interspersed throughout are words of wisdom (W.O.W.) from your peers. For the rest of the book, they'll be referred to as "W.O.W." because dental sleep medicine needs more acronyms. These are pearls from peeps with deep expertise and incisive viewpoints on relevant topics.

Read this book and practice its principles in all your affairs. Your patients, your team, and your pickleball partner will thank you for it. It works if you work it.

FIG. 1 "POSERS GOTTA PERISH"

POSERS GOTTA PERISH

"Lots of people want to be the noun without doing the verb. They want the job title without the work." —Austin Kleon

The journey to meaningful dental sleep medicine implementation and profitability is a lot like a gym membership. We've all seen gym ads adorned with toned, tanned gods and goddesses exhorting you to join them. Before-and-after photos showcase stunning beach bods. You can't help but gaze down shamefully at those extra pounds of COVID flab. You want what they've got. And it can be yours for a mere $19 a month for the six month introductory period.

In the real world, two-thirds of people who pony up for gym memberships never use them. After just six months, 22 percent stop going altogether, and 31 percent say that one year after joining a gym, they regretted the decision because it wasn't worth it. They didn't go enough and didn't put in the work, and so they didn't get the benefits they envisaged.

Some gyms have better equipment than others, and some have more skilled personal trainers, yummier smoothie bars, and cool gear for purchase. It doesn't matter what gym you join if you don't show up and do the work. Here's the thing: you still have to lift the weights. You still have to sweat. If you want to see the results, you have to drink those green smoothies even when you are at a Super Bowl party. There's no substitute. You can't sit on your La-Z-Boy, munching on Doritos and downing IPAs and complain that the gym doesn't work. It works. You don't.

The idea is laid out effectively in Ryan Holiday's seminal, *Ego Is the Enemy*. "Getting where we want to go isn't about brilliance; it's about sustained effort. It's not a sexy idea, but it's an encouraging one because it means that it's within everyone's reach."

This point cannot be stressed enough. Investor and entrepreneurial polymath Naval Ravikant drove the point home when he tweeted, "Doctors won't make you healthy. Nutritionists won't make you slim. Teachers won't make you smart. Gurus won't make you calm. Mentors won't make you rich. Trainers won't make you fit. Ultimately, you have to take responsibility. Save yourself."

Similarly, the secret to dental sleep success is no secret at all. It takes effort. Focus. Consistency. The right team. Falling down. Getting up. Learning. Applying what you've learned. Knocking on doors. Having doors slammed in your face and then knocking again. Repeat.

Others have done it before you, so you know it's possible. If you want to be a dental sleep medicine practitioner, the only way to make it happen is to practice dental sleep medicine.

Don't be a bitch. Make it happen.

YOU ACTUALLY PAID MONEY FOR THAT?

Are you going to be a specialist or a generalist? A dabbler? A do-it-all'er? What's your plan?

Bob Hoffman's *Advertising for Skeptics* notes that, "If you attend a lot of conferences as I do, you have undoubtedly noticed that speakers love to talk about the future. In fact, it's almost the only thing they ever talk about. Why? Because the present is too confusing, too complicated, and largely incomprehensible. But the future is great ... No one can fact-check the future. You can say anything you want, and people will think you are brilliant."

Hoffman's words resonate as so many lecturers paint a rosy picture of DSM's potential, potential they claim you can tap into only if you purchase their benefactor's products and services. There's an adage shared among sales reps in the field: "The only people making money in DSM are the speakers." This isn't entirely true, but it has the ring of truth and it's pretty damn funny.

There are good courses out there. The academic ones don't focus enough on how to treat more patients, and the commercial ones don't focus enough on the science. Why not get some of both? Consider some common sense criteria when choosing. If it's a commercial course, there will be commercials. You should hesitate before buying anything at the event. Go to another course first. You'll glean additional insights and get another commercial from a competitor of the host of the initial course. Again, don't buy anything.

Now go to an academic course and strike up conversations with fellow attendees. Find the two or three people who are actually treating 10 to 15 patients per month and share with them your experiences at the previous two courses. They'll give you something that resembles the truth. Then talk to the vendors about other companies' products. Some of those mofos will appear to have OD'd on truth serum. They'll tell you exactly what's up and whether the purchase you're considering is worth the money. Now you're equipped to make an informed buying decision. Alternatively, you can just call me—I'll give you the skinny.

Again, there are excellent courses you can attend, but there's also a lot of junk. If you get exposed to a glut of junk early, it will become foundational for you. You'll become like a baby born to a drug-addicted mother. This is how these contentious DSM tribes are formed. You have to be weaned off of it. You need to develop a healthy variety of educational inputs.

And just say "NO" to drugs.

W.O.W. BARRY GLASSMAN

Author's note: Dr. Barry Glassman is an iconoclastic stalwart in the DSM field. The world is his classroom, and his emphasis on evidence over emotions can rub some corporate interests the wrong way. I get it. He's one of my best friends, and he gives me a headache once a week. Sometimes it's because he's unwrapped the significance of new clinical research and other times it's because he's looking at received knowledge in ways some view as heretical. Other times it's due to a quip in an orthodontist's basement in Kansas. That's a story for another day.

—Jason Tierney

Toffler suggested that "the illiterate of the 20th century won't be those who can't read or write, but those who can't learn, unlearn, and relearn." Unlearning "facts" that have been cemented via confirmation bias is very difficult for us dentists whose basic training in the science did NOT include the scientific method. This is not our fault. It is the fault of dental education. So much of what we have learned is through empirical evidence; information handed down from previous generations of dentists that quite simply lacks any scientific validity. A non-responder with oral appliance therapy does not represent a clinical error on the dentist's part any more than a patient who doesn't respond to a specific drug represents a clinical error on the physician's part. Accepting this is critically important to success in dental sleep medicine.

Learning the principles of evidence-based medicine is the first step on a journey toward "truth." This knowledge leads to immediate skepticism of anecdotally based concepts. What gurus "believe" is not important. What matters is the preponderance of quality evidence.

Our goal is to create a patient-centric model based on good evidence that emphasizes conservative treatment and properly uses an intelligently based risk benefit decision quotient.

Incorporating the philosophical tenets of Miguel Ruiz's *Four Agreements* has proven to be extremely helpful in a positive change to a better practice model. Learning to be impeccable with your word and truly honest with patients while setting appropriate expectations makes the practice of dental sleep medicine nearly stress-free and ultimately much more rewarding. Learning to listen to patients and not to take anything personally, not making assumptions about others, and doing your best all contribute to a healthy attitude, improved patient and physician relationships, and an increased ability to guide your patients to their best potential outcomes without fear of failure.

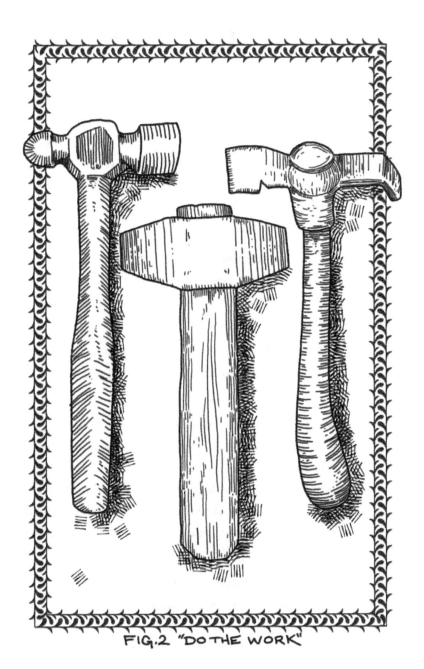

FIG. 2 "DO THE WORK"

THE 100 CLUB

In 2015, Frost and Sullivan, a respected market research firm, published a report on the state of the sleep field and its forecast for the next five years—basically where we are today. In their report, the data crunchers noted that only 100 dentists—what we'll call "The 100 Club"—were responsible for approximately 32 percent of the custom appliances prescribed in the U.S. each year. It also divined that, by the time you read this, more than 3 million appliances would be delivered annually.

Lo and behold, this has not happened. They missed the bullseye. Hell, they missed the entire target. As of this book's writing in 2023, the ADA estimates the number of general dentists in the U.S. at 185,000. This means the other 184,900 have their work cut out for them.

Who are these dentists? The participants in dental sleep hokey-pokey usually conform to one of these character profiles. See if you identify with any of them.

- **Dr. Ireada Studythatsaid:** This dentist yearns to know everything about sleep medicine, except, you know, how to actually provide sleep medicine procedures in their practice. They rack up dozens of hours of CE, debate the ethics of medical billing, deliberate over which appliance would have been better indicated for a patient they read about in some obscure case study, and suck the minds and resources dry from every sales rep who will take their calls.

  You have to commend this type's commitment to lifelong learning. Oftentimes, those of Dr. Studythatsaid's ilk are also amateur engineers. They love to wax philosophical with sales reps about how they should reconfigure their devices because, "One time I saw a poster presentation by a guy who treated a patient who ..." I used to run into these guys a lot and, well, I'm just glad we were never near a high enough balcony.

- **Dr. Juggler:** They are eager to provide the best care possible, and they grasp the benefits of adding sleep to the practice. But. They. Just. Can't. Find. The. Time. This manifests as unused HST units and drawers filled with disposables, untrained teams, and unscreened patients. It nearly always results in total abandonment of the DSM mission. They are usually up to their eyeballs in busyness, but at least it's in procedures they're intimately familiar with. They earn a decent living and go home, but they aren't happy. They suffer from the discomfort of being comfortable. Their velvet handcuffs are getting too tight.

Implementing DSM into your practice isn't an all-or-nothing proposition. If you provide Invisalign or another clear aligner solution, you didn't go to a 24 month ortho program, and if you're a general dentist placing implants, you didn't enroll in an oral surgery residency.

You can have multiple goals and focuses. However, if you are spread too thin, balance and accomplishments will elude you. In *Winning*, Tim Grover, author and former personal trainer to Michael Jordan, Kobe Bryant, and other elite athletes, deftly compares too many goals and inputs to GPS. He says it's like simultaneously putting your destination into Google Maps, Waze, and MapQuest. Each will take you on a different route, with a different ETA. It's unnecessarily confusing. Just don't do it.

- **Dr. Ima Holdup:** Don't confuse Dr. Holdup with Dr. Juggler. Dr. Holdup insists on being involved in every step of the dental sleep implementation process despite being chronically double-booked and ten minutes behind. They refuse to let the team go to a medical billing seminar without being there personally. They have to do all the sleep consults, discuss financial arrangements, and be present for all sleep team training. Dr. Holdup's micro-management style strips the team of any sense of autonomy. This doctor doesn't delegate or grant latitude, hindering progress at every turn. They're the bottleneck every time.

- **Chris Plateau, DDS, D-ABDSM, D-ASBA:** Dr. Plateau treats more sleep patients than most dentists, usually in the 2-to-10 patients per month range. They might even lecture around the country teaching other dentists how to replicate their success. This looks great until you consider that they live in a town of 400,000. Statistically, about 100,000 of them probably have obstructive sleep apnea (OSA). At this rate, they'll treat them all in 833 years.

  Also, consider how this doc earned their namesake. While the patient volume may seem desirable and it's certainly much more than most do before they quit, they've been stalled at this number for years. They're too busy protecting their ego and living the DSM high life to approach the field with the open mind that got them to this point.

  New marketing avenues and physician referral sources, and a new outlook would likely accelerate their practice so they can join the aforementioned 100 Club. But who cares when everyone fawns over them at the AADSM annual meeting's happy hour? Geezus Louizus.

If you're one of these people, that's OK. Our worst traits are nearly always our most desirable ones that have been allowed to run amok.

Dialing back Dr. Studythatsaid's analytical nature a bit makes him an extremely conscientious clinician who wants to do all he can to give his patient the best treatment.

Focusing Dr. Juggler's unending energy on a few key targets will transform them into a powerhouse.

And setting new goals for Dr. Plateau can help them become Dr. Peaks. You get the idea.

IT'S ALL BEEN DONE
BEFORE

I've been haranguing you about doing the work, but it's not because I'm a taskmaster. It's because the avoidance of the work deteriorates into unrealized dreams. That's why so many wannabe authors fail to publish books, and it's why aspiring martial artists can be found on the couch watching *Beverly Hills Ninja* while drowning their hopes in Mountain Dew and Flamin' Hot Cheetos. And it's where prospective dental sleep game-changers default back to "too busy," "insurance doesn't pay," and so on and so on.

Medical codes exist for oral appliance therapy, so you get reimbursed for your time and expertise. The ADA, AADSM, AASM, and other professional organizations support dentists' role in identifying and treating sleep disordered breathing.

Home sleep testing technology and precision medical devices have evolved tremendously in just the past decade.

Others have already blazed the trails. They've beaten down the path so you can go further, faster, and with less effort. Nearly 500 years ago, Niccolo Machiavelli wrote that, "a prudent man should always enter by the paths beaten by great men and imitate those who have been most excellent, so that, if his own skill does not come up to theirs, at least it will give off something of the odor of theirs."

Kent Smith has a thriving standalone sleep practice. So do Stacey Layman and Max Kerr. Erin Elliott treats a ton of sleep patients in her restorative dental practice. Jason Doucette and John Tucker do, too. They've done it, so we know it can be done. If *they* can do it, so can you. The ancient philosopher Marcus Aurelius nails the point concisely in his *Meditations*. More than two millennia ago, he wrote, "Do not think that what is hard for you is humanly impossible; and if it is humanly possible, consider it to be within reach."

We don't have to start from zero, and it doesn't have to be perfect; we just have to start. Voltaire spoke to this point 300 years ago when he wrote, "Perfect is the enemy of good" and the Gorilla Biscuits drove it home when they screamed, "Start today!" We stand on the shoulders of giants. Let's build on the knowledge, wisdom, and experience they've gifted us. GO!

DSM – DENTAL SLEEP MINEFIELD

Dental sleep medicine is a minefield ensconced within an obstacle course, but the mines can be cleared, and the obstacle is the way.

How do I know? Because I've seen dozens of dentists do it, and they live incredibly rewarding lives. They've attained that elusive work/life balance. These dentists enjoy enviable incomes and fulfilling careers with plenty of time for family and their other pursuits. From golf to gardening and scuba diving to ultramarathons, they are living fully.

I've worked with thousands of dentists, but I just referenced the "dozens" who have made it work. That's not a typo. That's the truth. The cold, hard truth.

Do you want to know how they arrived at the promised land?

SPOILER ALERT: it isn't because they picked the "right appliance."

On that note, allow me to digress about appliances and DSM in general. Maybe you used a TAP, or SomnoMed Avant, or ProSomnus EVO Select once before and the patient "didn't like it." Perhaps you "tried DSM before, but it didn't work" (whatever that means). That doesn't mean you should give up.

Imagine you decide to try a gyro from Elias's favorite Greek joint and you don't like it. Are you going to swear off food and starve to death? Of course not. Maybe this example seems ludicrous. It should. Maybe it seems like a non sequitur. It isn't.

I managed operations for a leading DSM software company, and I heard some version of the following story *ad infinitum*. A dentist signs up for the service at a CE event. Our team reaches out to the practice repeatedly to schedule training. My colleagues call, email, leave messages, and send texts. Many practices don't actually participate in training, nor do they seriously screen their patients, send letters to physicians, or schedule consultations with patients. We could actually monitor this in their software.

After about six months of floundering and a couple dozen pings from our team, the dentist calls and demands a refund because "The software doesn't work."

"Dr. Dumass, would you mind telling me more, please?"

"Yeah, the guy that sold me the software said it was gonna be so easy, and we'd see a bunch of patients, but it just doesn't work. We never got trained, and the software doesn't work."

"Dr. Dumass," I would begin, reading from my mental script, "I sold you the software at the course in Arizona, and I recall very clearly telling you how much energy and focus this would require. My colleagues also conveyed that same message to your team when they called. It looks like they sent 26 emails and spoke with Jennifer 15 times and had an initial training session with Brittany. During the subsequent 13 calls, she declined to schedule the next training session because she was too busy and didn't understand why you signed up for this in the first place. Looking at your software, it doesn't appear that any patients were screened or entered into the system, nor has anyone from your team logged in since that initial training. Does this sound about right? I'll give you a refund, but can you help me understand how the 'software didn't work,' Dr. Dumass? Dr. Dumass? Are you there?"

Allow me to connect the dots for you. One minor lackluster experience isn't a good reason to swear off an entire field.

W.O.W. JASON DOUCETTE

Author's note: Dr. Jason Doucette is a busy general dentist in Reno, Nevada. He places a lot of implants, creates beautiful smiles, and he's helped countless patients sleep better and live healthier lives. Dr. Doucette is one of the most sincere, genuine, kind people I've ever known, and I'm honored to count him as a friend. —Jason Tierney

While in the throes of a 15-year love affair with implant dentistry and full mouth esthetics, I was introduced to the "foreign" world of dental sleep medicine. Little did I know that this routine CE trip to a Sleep Group Solutions course at Glidewell Dental Laboratory would "wreck" my entire professional paradigm and set me on an entirely new path and passion in dentistry…

My team and I began to screen and treat a few team members and their spouses. Once we saw what we were able to do for those people closest to us by improving their quality of life and saving lives —the journey began, and I knew what I wanted to do for the rest my career.

In the beginning, I wasn't sure if DSM just be another part of my general dental practice, or if it could grow to become a true "specialty practice" of its own? Due to the high prevalence of obstructive sleep apnea in our little Reno, Nevada community, we have had multiple full time dental sleep medicine assistants seeing DSM patients all day long, every day, for more than five years.

I'm now up against the challenge of trying to keep up with doing dentistry full-time in the face of a successful full-time DSM practice. Most dental sleep medicine practices are run similar to an orthodontic practice. In this setting, the dental team does much of the "hands-on" work within the allowable parameters of each state's dental statutes and the doctor does all the treatment planning, decision making, and "hands-on" treatment where legally indicated. However, imagine having two more additional "hygiene columns" or "dental emergency columns" full of new and existing patients in your already busy dental schedule that you need to address on an hourly basis. It's a lot! I refer to it as "The Struggle of the Juggle!"

Mark my words, there is no community large or small, rural, urban, or suburban with a shortage of people of all ages suffering from sleep breathing disorders. Any dentist screening and treating DSM patients in their practice, will surely experience exponential growth in production, new patients, team members, and most importantly, professional satisfaction, far beyond anything bread and butter dentistry has ever offered.

General dentistry is a very hands-on game in most practices while dental sleep medicine is really a thinking dentist's game. This is the time to ask yourself some questions and really consider the options: what is your vision and what do you want? Because if you get "bit" by the proverbial "sleep bug", you will quickly find yourself enveloped by "the struggle of the juggle."

Have a vision for what you want to do because remaining in the "the juggle" too long may prove to be challenging beyond what many would consider effectively workable and enjoyable.

To reduce the struggle and make the juggle more manageable, create and run your DSM practice through a separate LLC, use a DSM software, contract with a reputable third-party medical billing service, acquire the necessary technology, and most importantly, find team "champions" in your office to implement and help run your DSM practice. You can do this. You should do this. Your community needs you.

DSM MATTERS

Dental sleep medicine is challenging. If your goal is to generate $2 million per year in your general dentistry practice and another couple million in sleep medicine, it's probably not going to happen. DSM takes time. It also takes dedication and focused critical thinking.

More than 30 million Americans have obstructive sleep apnea. You've heard that number or read a similar one. It's usually followed by some marketing pronouncement that all those patients are going to need appliances from you. This is where I want to do that coughing "BULLSHIT!" sneeze thing.

OSA is a problem, a big one, and patients need help. Dentists are uniquely positioned to provide that help. Please note that I said "dentists," not "dentistry." That's intentional. Dentistry is a slow-moving bureaucratic behemoth of a profession. It's akin to a gigantic barge, with each section beholden to some special interest. Try turning that around in a timely fashion.

Dentists like you have the flexibility and latitude to help people, and even save lives, and make a great living in the process. Compared to that unwieldy barge, your practice is a nimble skiff, and you are the captain.

NOW IS THE TIME

"The future starts today, not tomorrow." — *Pope John Paul II*

"I'm going to start incorporating a sleep program after I hire a new office manager and my assistant comes back from maternity leave."

"Once I'm treating five patients each month, then I'll invest in hiring a sleep champion."

"I can't justify the expense of sleep software to simplify workflow until I have enough patients."

Sound familiar? At first glance, these objections all make sense, and they probably seemed reasonable when you uttered them to a salesperson, lecturer, or consultant. However, we have *Rework* authors Jason Fried and David Heinemeier Hansson's infinite wisdom to correct us: "The perfect time never arrives. You're always too young or old or busy or broke or something else. If you constantly fret about timing things perfectly, they'll never happen."

Eventually you'll find a new office manager who'll be better than any you've ever had before. Maybe the assistant won't return from maternity leave. One of your hygienists will quit. Life rolls on. New challenges will arise. The *only* perfect time is now, and now will never happen again.

Once you jump out of the nest, you'll figure out how to fly. Your first chamfer prep took all day. Now you do it half-awake while daydreaming about working three days per week and seeing only sleep patients.

FIG.3 "MAKE TIME"

MAKE TIME, NOT EXCUSES

"I wish I had the time to [do whatever], but [INSERT BULLSHIT EXCUSE HERE]."
"I definitely want to start [doing whatever], but I just don't have the time."

Other people make time. They achieve 10 times the success in just 10 percent of the time. Time is a scarce, non-renewable resource. We can't actually *make time,* of course, but we can certainly make excuses. We're experts at making excuses for why we can't do things. In this realm, we're incredibly resourceful and imaginative. And it's not just you. The resistance afflicts everyone. The person you want to be battles the resistance, and the barriers to success reach new heights. The high achiever you aspire to be allocates their time cautiously and acts intentionally so they can do the things they want to do.

In his *New York Times* bestseller, *Four Thousand Weeks: Time Management for Mortals,* Oliver Burkeman gives us this dose of reality: "I would never succeed in marshaling enough efficiency, self-discipline, and effort to force my way through to the feeling that I was on top of everything, that I was fulfilling all my obligations and had no need to worry about the future." Surrendering to this reality is liberating. It's like an alcoholic admitting that they're powerless over alcohol.

It's true. The time is never right. I've heard so much well-intentioned self-deception from dentists on the topic of DSM implementation or leveling-up their sleep practices. There will be competing demands for your time and attention until the day you croak. There will be no pause for you to put everything in its perfect place. You'll have to make time for what matters. Most of the time, we're pulling the wool over our own eyes. We believe the stories we tell ourselves because we've repeated them so often. The calls are coming from inside the house. I was afflicted with the same ailment. That's why it took me so long to get this book into your hands.

There's a Chinese proverb that's relevant here: "The best time to plant a tree was 20 years ago. The second best time is now."

Are you open to a second order change? Can we agree to stop with the charades and get to work? It's time.

SLEEP IS LIKE GENERAL DENTISTRY ... BUT DIFFERENT

As with most issues in the world, we can probably get further if we first acknowledge the things we have in common. Sure, there are differences, too, but that's what makes life interesting.

Dental sleep medicine is kinda like that. It has much in common with general dentistry. You rely on your team to make things happen, and so the team had better be strong. It's the same with DSM. The responsibilities change, but everyone has a role, and they need to perform at a high level, or the ejection seat will launch them elsewhere.

You already refer patients to specialists such as periodontists and oral surgeons. With DSM, you'll usually be referring to physicians. Your patient health history forms ask about the history of tobacco use. You conduct oral cancer exams as the standard of care. If you see anything concerning, you refer for a biopsy. So, why wouldn't it be the standard of care to ask about sleep on your health history forms, conduct a visual screening for SDB, and refer for a sleep test as warranted?

Before you start citing outdated hearsay from your golf buddy who heard something from someone at a study club five years ago that DSM is outside your scope of practice, let me assure you that you, as a general dentist, can and (according to the ADA) *should* screen your patients for SDB. And when it's appropriate, you should treat them, too.

This isn't an all-or-nothing proposition, and it needn't be a situation where you sell your practice and go all-in on this sleep deal. You don't have to abandon hygiene checks tomorrow so you can get triple board-certified in sleep. When you bought a CBCT unit, you didn't get accredited as a radiology tech before taking a scan. No, you took some courses. You learned. You got hands-on experience. You learned some more. And you kept doing it until you achieved proficiency. The more you did, the more proficient you became. The more proficient you became, the more prolific you became. The more prolific you became, the more you enjoyed it. And the more you enjoyed it, the more profitable it became.

As Dr. John Tucker says, "Dental sleep medicine isn't hard. It's different."

THE GENERALIST DENTIST

A phalanx of dentists gallivants from town to town on the lecture circuit. Like paunchy carnival barkers they bellow, "Drink the Kool-Aid, and you too, can treat 200 new sleep patients every month."

Three days per week? No emergency appointments? Adoration of the medical community? Raving fans and piles of huge EOBs? You're enthralled by the possibilities.

But there's one pesky thing – you're a general dentist with a general dentistry practice. That lecturer, Dr. Libel, has been exclusively treating sleep for as long as you've been outta school, man. Plus, he only reached that patient volume once in twenty years, and the amount of that EOB was an anomaly – three times the average he normally sees.

Don't cry, dry your eyes. There's still a blue ocean of opportunity for you. But don't believe the hype. Take what you need from that speaker and leave the rest. Pick up some pearls about how to position the patient's payment responsibility. Marry it to your own excellent case presentation skills.

At the next lecture, grab some gems on initial starting position and pair that with your TMJ knowledge. Read a journal article on the prevalence of OSA in hospital settings and ponder what those stats mean for your own restorative patients. What about that *USA Today* article you read on the importance of sleep? How can you optimize that piece to increase awareness among your patients and spark conversations about snoring and sleep apnea?

More than 40 years ago, Steve Jobs opined, "If you're gonna make connections which are innovative, you have to not have the same bag of experience everyone else has." Develop a deep foundational knowledge and draw from your wide range of experiences and influences. Theory coupled with practice turns to knowledge. Add some time and humility to the equation, and you're on the road to becoming a wise DSM practitioner. If you don't do this, you're inclined to trip over yourself trying to mimic Dr. Libel.

The broad and deep experience combo is key to create exciting change. As a general dentist, you're fluent in patient management, referring to specialists, and anatomy. If you aren't already knowledgeable about sleep, you can obtain a foundational knowledge base pretty quickly. However, you aren't blinded by hospital systems, typical medical treatment pathways, and the ennui some of your medical colleagues have fallen prey to. You have a fresh set of eyes to survey the landscape and see things anew.

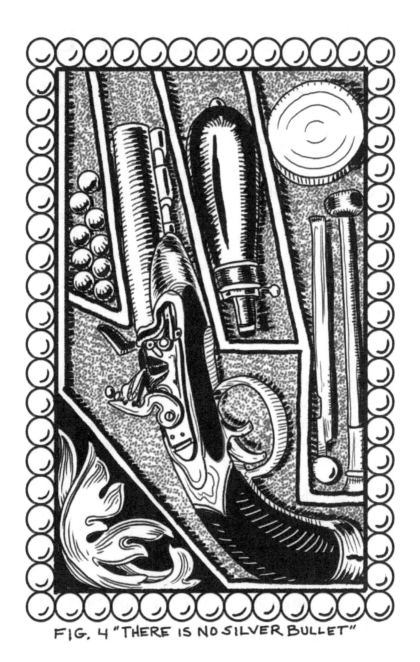

FIG. 4 "THERE IS NO SILVER BULLET"

YOU CAN BUY LOVE,
BUT YOU CAN'T BUY THIS

"There are no silver bullets, only lead ones." — Ben Horowitz

This endeavor is not for the faint of heart. DSM is a graveyard of get-rich-quick schemes. It's not that you can't get rich, but it won't happen quickly. And it won't be hard, but it won't be easy either.

These pages contain the truth, maybe not the only truth, but the truth, nonetheless. This book will give you what you need, which may not be what you want. There's a difference. You *want* a quick, easy, pain-free path, but what you *need* is a pathway illuminated by unbiased honesty and lived experience.

The book you're holding will give you what you need to build a healthy sleep practice. It's a big-ass sweet potato, loaded with nutrients and vitamins that will help you. You'd probably prefer Sweet-Tarts. The junk that feels good in the near term, but it doesn't help you, and it may even hurt you in the long run.

NEWS FLASH! There's no way to buy your way to dental sleep success. There are companies claiming that you can write them a check and they'll share a proprietary secret plan with you, a veritable treasure map even. Those are falsehoods. They're lying. It's a contract for a cult. I went to some of these companies' meetings and spent time with their principals. I solicited input from their clients, both those who claimed they'd attained a state of blissful DSM nirvana and those who filed lawsuits, alleging theft and fraud. Pro athletes aren't going the slam dunk for DSM riches.

It was hard to understand how groups that some identified as the reason for their success could be viewed by so many others as scammers. To learn more, I read books such as Eric Hoffer's *The True Believer*, *Propaganda* by Edward Bernays, *Cultish* by Amanda Montell, and Haruki Murakami's *Underground*. None of these books are related to building businesses, delivering optimal patient care, or standardizing dental practice management. They're about cults. Films like *The Tinder Swindler* and *Bad Vegan* can help connect the dots. The details are different and the characters change, but the scams selling dreams that are really nightmares stand in stark relief.

Megan Goodwin, a Northwestern University researcher, warns that, "The political ramifications of identifying something as a cult are real and often violent." If I disappear, it was probably one of the DSM scam cults.

Their promise of an OAT-lined autobahn is in reality a fast-track to disappointment, missed opportunities, and, if you aren't careful, financial ruin and legal woes. I've witnessed enough of them. Don't slow down, and don't crane your neck. Keep moving. Nothing to see here. Switch lanes.

I've had this conversation with numerous dentists on multiple occasions. Most of the time they trust their gut and my suggestion was just the nudge they needed to walk (RUN) away from the scammers. However, a few ignored my warning and gave in to the promise of easy money. Eventually, we cross paths again, and without fail, these well-intentioned dentists admit to having been fleeced. I'm bummed for them. They wasted time, goodwill, and good money.

I FEEL YOUR PAIN

"How do you know where I'm at if you haven't been where I've been; understand where I'm coming from?" — B-Real of Cypress Hill

Do you contract with a third-party biller, stick with a fee-for-service model, or hire a medical biller? I'm telling you, work with a third-party biller—but which one? You make a few calls, and they all give you different information and say that they're the best.

Lo and behold, one of the companies claims to possess the golden ticket to getting consistently high reimbursement with minimal hassle. Their fees seem pricey, but if they really do hold the secret, it's a small investment for a huge return. And if it's really a turnkey solution, it's worth every dime. You're assured that they've seen it all, and for a pittance, they'll do all the heavy lifting for you. The appeal is strong. Their sales pitch feels a bit yucky, but their confidence is infectious. These guys provide false clarity in a new landscape of uncertainty. Unfortunately, the path is rife with pitfalls and slithering snakes.

I'm not a dentist, but I know what you're going through. Check it out: I've never published a book before, and I'm no Shakespeare, but I can craft a sentence. I started writing the book you're reading now, and it was moving along at a decent clip.

Eventually, I had to decide which platform I should use to publish the book. That decision tree branched into questions about cover artists, designs, page size, paper color, keywords, pricing strategies, review processes, copyediting—the list goes on.

Every one of these questions sparked more decisions until, finally, it felt like a decision tree forest fire. The resultant smokescreen caused starts, stops, and pauses, which I falsely attributed to my day job and family life. I didn't want to make the wrong decisions, and so I made the worst decision of all: to do nothing.

The page-count didn't add up, but the excuses did. Each time I sat down to write, it got harder. There had to be an easier way—a better way. This quest led me to discover that

the turnkey quackery isn't unique to dental sleep medicine. When searching for accomplished, trustworthy cover designers, I uncovered those who claimed they could also do the page layout and even the editing. This last one was laughable given the artist's English skills evidenced in our email correspondence. "I edit book 4 u and do cover of book no worries you will so happy five stars."

"GEEZ LOUISE," I thought, "these charlatans hoodwink authors, too."

I ran and ran on the publishing treadmill, trying to figure everything out. Instead of writing, I researched how to do all the ancillary tasks associated with publishing a book that looked increasingly less likely ever to get finished because I was sinking in the morass of researching how to publish a damn book. It's a vicious cycle. Sound familiar?

Eureka! Just like DSM, the book publishing world hosts a ring of hell, featuring slick marketers, proclaiming that they can do it all for you. It costs a sizable chunk of change, but it's worth the investment, they say. Remember, it'll all be done for you. There are lots of these companies, and they all sound so promising. I watched their webinars, downloaded their free e-books, and subscribed to their email newsletters. I got some pointers from their content and appreciated their pearls. I even liked some of the presenters. I'd read some of their books, but the closer I got to making a purchase, the clearer the pattern became.

It's the same in DSM. We're told they'll do it all for us, and it gives us a sense of solace until the credit card is swiped. Then it's more like the scene from *National Lampoon's Vacation*, when the Griswolds stop to ask for directions while rolling the Family Truckster through the notoriously blighted streets of East St. Louis.

CLARK. We're from out of town.

GROVER. No shit?

CLARK. Listen, I'd really appreciate it if you could give me directions back onto the expressway.

GROVER. What? For free? Five dollars.

CLARK. I'm not going to give you money for directions!

ELLEN. I think that's fair, Clark.

CLARK. OK. Here's five dollars. Keep the change.

GROVER. You see which way you're pointing? You see that place? Do you see the sign, "Rib Tips?" Well, f*ck that, you don't want to go that way. You go half a block down the street, and you'll see a Torino with no wheels on it. Inside that Torino is my cousin, Jackie. Tell him that you're my boy and that you're lost. He'll make sure you get where you're going. You don't want to know from me. I'm not from this neighborhood. I'm from the west side of Chicago, here on vacation.

There are no shortcuts to success. You have to do the work.

SUPPLEMENTS VERSUS SUBSTITUTES

Too many dentists try to buy their way to DSM success. This isn't a CEREC problem. You can't just purchase an in-office miller and somehow treat more sleep patients. Subscribing to the right billing service or getting the right home sleep testing (HST) interpretation service is going to be the game-changer.

How do you know which home sleep testing unit is best? Easy, it's the one the sales guy you're talking to is selling. Guess which billing company is best? You guessed it. It's the company the rep you're talking to works for.

There are several excellent sleep testing units, and you can—and should—compare features, pricing, and so on. There are a couple of exceptional billing companies out there, too. You should definitely evaluate their pros and cons and consider how they might work with your practice. But don't think for one second that picking the right HST unit, medical billing company, or appliance manufacturer will catapult you into the dental sleep practice stratosphere.

These tools are like vitamin supplements. Selecting the right ones may enhance your performance, but they aren't substitutes. Multivitamins might provide health benefits, but you can't eat them in lieu of meals. That's just not how it works, and it's the same with DSM equipment.

Purchasing the "right" gadget or subscribing to a certain software package will not get you into the 100 Club of DSM providers. These things might help you work more efficiently, but you still have to perform the services. None of them will guarantee success. Similarly, streamlined HST protocols might reduce costs and help you see more patients diagnosed. A good billing company will help you minimize denials and simplify processes.

Aligning with best-in-class partners is certainly necessary, but you can't buy the same TaylorMade wedge Tiger Woods uses and suddenly chip 110 yards out of the sand directly into the hole. Tiger Woods could take a wiffle ball bat or grab some clubs from the thrift store and shoot a round below par.

Don't make things needlessly difficult on yourself. Use the right tools, but always remember: supplements are not substitutes.

FIG. 5 "SAVE LIVES, MAKE MONEY"

WHAT ARE YOU ASHAMED OF?

Years ago, I kicked off a CE presentation by asking everyone to "raise your hands if you screen all your patients for oral cancer." Each hand went up. Every one of them.

"How many of you with your hands up have detected a lesion in the past 12 months?" Nearly every hand went down. Out of 30 dentists, just two hands stayed up.

My next question: "Either of you detected more than one squamous cell carcinoma in the past year?" Both hands went down.

Then I asked the audience why they screened *every single one of their adult patients* for something that affected just .0001 percent of adult Americans. Several people answered like there was a free trip to Fiji on the line, "Because we're in the oral cavity already. We care for our patients, and this could save their lives. And it's the standard of care in our practice."

Continuing my enquiry, "Show of hands one more time: how many of you screen all of your adult patients for sleep disordered breathing?" Only three hands went up this time. That was actually more than usual.

"How many of you with your hands up have detected at least one patient with sleep disordered breathing in the past year?" All three hands remained up.

"How many of you have seen at least five in the past year?" They chuckled. "I saw five *yesterday!*" one dentist exclaimed.

The other two chimed in with similar observations. "Yup, big-ass tongue on one, and the other couldn't wear her CPAP."

The crowd-participation portion of the session continued when I asked why they screen their patients for sleep disordered breathing. Like the answer was glaringly obvious, Dr. Five scoffed, "Just like oral cancer screenings; we're in the mouth already. We care about our patients, and it can be deadly. We can do something about it. It's the standard of care in our practice."

I could see the light bulbs lighting up. The room was aglow with the DSM holy spirit. Heads nodded. To drive the message home, I said, "Admirably, everyone in here is screening their patients for a potentially deadly disease that impacts far less than 1 percent of the population. You're doing this because you're altruistic. You care about your patients. You're in their mouths already and it's the standard of care. Discovering something and referring a patient for a biopsy could save their lives. Is that correct?"

Heads nodded. Absolutely. Amen. Preach, *Brother Jason*.

"There's another disease that affects 25 percent of the population. You can screen for it easily and identify signs of it in the oral cavity. You care about your patients, and this could save their lives. According to the ADA, it's the standard of care. So why aren't you doing it?"

Silence. I could hear the mental wheels turning as they chewed on this food for thought. "One more question for the three of you who are screening all your patients for sleep disordered breathing: Are there any other reasons you screen those patients?"

Again, the room went silent, but it was a different kind of silence, the silence of sheepishness. Uncertainty. Trepidation about giving the wrong answer. It was second grade all over again. Like that sadistic teacher everyone dreads, I called on one of the three whose hands were still up. "Any other reasons, Doctor? You care about your patients. It's the standard of care. You're in the oral cavity so this is in your scope of practice. What else?"

One dentist muttered something. Maybe it wasn't a dentist at all. She sounded more like a church mouse; she was so quiet.

"What was that?" I asked, leaning forward like I was trying to hear the intermittent sound the car isn't supposed to be making. Listen. Did you hear that? Shhhh…

"Mooblysh", she stammered. At least that's what it sounded like.

"Can you repeat that, Doctor?"

Grudgingly, she said, "Money. It can be very profitable." She was opening up, and her confidence increased as she spoke, "It takes so little of my time, we get paid really well for it, and I actually enjoy doing it. The response from patients is unlike anything else. And like I said, we get reimbursed really well in some cases."

That's what I was looking for.

In no other business are people so ashamed about wanting to make money. Athletes aren't. Rappers definitely aren't. Even religious institutions aren't. Why are you?

Dental sleep medicine is about caring for patients, but it's still a business, and when done right, it can be a very profitable one. It's a vocation. Commit to it. Otherwise, you're just an amateur. Maybe it's not for you, and maybe that's OK (not really—patients need you!), but it's important that you be honest with yourself now. Consider why you're involved in dental sleep medicine. It's just you and your reflection in the mirror. You can tell the world whatever tale you want, but be honest with yourself. Why are you doing this?

Let's run through an exercise that might help you. Force rank the following reasons for DSM in your practice, with 1 the most important and 7 the least important:

_____ **Help my patients**

_____ **Should be the standard of care**

_____ **Seems interesting**

_____ **Increase revenue**

_____ **Have a personal story or know someone who does**

_____ **Differentiate the practice**

_____ **Other**

If you ranked "Increase revenue" "1" or "2," you'll probably flounder, fail, and bail. Don't waste your time, energy, or money going along for the ride. Go get on the clear aligner bus.

In his brilliant *War of Art,* Steven Pressfield writes, "Technically, the professional takes money. Technically the professional plays for pay. But in the end, he does it for love."

That's you. You're a professional. Keep reading.

You just might save lives and make a lot of money.

If that last sentence bothered you, read it again and get comfortable with it.

DAVID VS. GOLIATH – A DSM TALE

Dentists all over the country face pressure from dental service organizations (DSO). In 2017, a mere 7.4 percent of dental practices were associated with a DSO. DSOs grew by a whopping 40 percent over the following three years. Some forecasts estimate that, by 2030, nearly 80 percent of practices will be affiliated with a DSO or similar managed organization.

If you haven't already sold out, you might be queuing up the quote from Dante's *Inferno*: "Abandon hope all ye who enter here." DSOs have resources, experience, and efficient marketing schemes. They drive prices down. They poach patients. They're with every insurance plan and turn once loyal patients into practice-hoppers. Many of your colleagues feel that these organizations extract the fulfillment and profitability out of dentistry while injecting fear and loathing into the sulcus that was once your career.

This is where you step in with a vision, conviction, and a strategic action plan. You won't need a slingshot though. You're not going to slay the DSOs. You aren't even going to think about them ever again. Grab some s'mores and gather 'round the fire, kids. I have a story to tell.

A friend of mine, let's call him "Dr. Conan," is a renowned DSM educator. He has one of the most prolific sleep practices in the country. At the time this story took place, Dr. Conan was treating around 80 sleep patients every month. He's the real deal.

At one of his lectures, the dentist owner of a burgeoning 10-office group practice approached Dr. Conan, waxing excitedly about his desire to implement DSM in all his offices. Dr. C had heard this one before. DSO representatives were frequently waiting in the wings after his presentations.

Most of them fell into one of two categories: Either they claimed a strong interest in implementing but bailed after wasting everyone's time, or they snidely disclosed all the ill-informed reasons why DSM is a bad business case for dental practices.

But this guy was different. He expressed his willingness to put real money on the line. Dr. Conan signed on to help the group implement a DSM program involving its 50 dentists and 10 locations. Much to his wife's chagrin, the group's offices were located two time zones away, so some travel was necessitated but much of the training could be done over Zoom.

Dr. Conan is a student of the psychology of teams, an authority on the powers of persuasion, and a specialist on sundry learning behaviors. Still, after three months of online training via Zoom calls, workbooks, and even two weeks of embedded training at the offices, the resulting growth was underwhelming.

You won't believe what he did next. Dr. Conan restructured his contract with the DSO and uprooted his entire family to move to across the country, where the group's offices were located. He worked full-time in the practice: training, coaching, doing hands-on demonstrations, and even treating some patients himself.

One year into the relationship, the owner scheduled a review session. Dr. C entered the meeting expecting to be dealt the first business failure of his enviable career. His eyes widened and his brow furrowed as the owner gleefully proclaimed that the offices had finally surpassed the 100 treated patients per month metric. His alacrity was in stark contrast to Dr. Conan's disappointment.

Dr. Conan informed the owner matter-of-factly that he was treating nearly 100 patients by himself back home. After a full year of total immersion with the group, their 50 dentists in 10 locations were doing about the same he did solo.

Flabbergasted, I asked Dr. C what he learned from the experience. His response is tattooed on my brain.

"Jason, dental sleep is antithetical to the DSO model, which is totally reliant on transactional patient experiences. It is process, not purpose driven. Because of this, a focused, smart, caring owner practitioner will beat the DSO all day, every day. That dentist will build a medical referral base, earn patient referrals, and treat patients right, and the collections will grow. That's the message dentists need to hear. When it comes to dental sleep, David will beat Goliath every time."

In Peter Thiel's must-read *Zero to One,* the PayPal and Palantir co-founder writes, "Superior sales and distribution by itself can create a monopoly, even with no product differentiation. The converse is not true." The takeaway is that, if you provide compassionate, high-quality care and deliver value consistently, you will separate yourself from the appliance delivery docs and the DSOs. You are not a commodity. You are irreplaceable.

W.O.W. KENT SMITH

Author's note: Dr. Kent Smith has built one of — if not THE —most prodigious sleep practices in the world, showing us all what possibility looks like. He's a novelist and a revered lecturer. Dr. Smith is also an accomplished scuba diver, doting father, and the founder of the annual Sleep Roundtable meeting in Dallas. Oh, and he looks dapper in a fedora.
—*Jason Tierney*

Aside from medical billing, which has been chronicled extensively as the number-one hurdle, I have become convinced that the most elusive trait that leads to success is the ability and willingness to embrace change. This characteristic has many tentacles, which I will attempt to cover in a few words.

- Let's begin with your help-wanted ad. I prefer sleep team members with no dental experience. Having a team member pulled away to help the dentist with a composite is the death knell for sleep growth.

- Delegation is key. Many dentists already struggle with this in the dental world, but medicine almost demands it. Considerable delegation is permitted and should be championed. States vary with the scope of delegation, but ideally, you would sidle up to the boundary and make nice.

- Communicate extensively. This is a paradigm change for the majority of dentists. We were not taught in dental school to send letters to health care practitioners listed on the health histories of our patients.

This is particularly true for any provider who refers a patient to you. If you never want that doctor to refer to you again, then don't send a note explaining how you treated your common patient.

- Change your concept of occlusion. I have heard my share of dentists who decide not to pursue dental sleep medicine because it goes against whatever occlusion camp gave them a diploma. Bites will change. A Class III Angle position has never caused a stroke. Lack of oxygen during sleep can.

- If you plan on transitioning eventually to a sleep-only practice, you will need to change your perception of how you rank among the dental elite. Many dentists think, perhaps rightfully so, that no other dentist could treat their patients with the skill and compassion with which they were blessed. If this reverberates, it's time to, as Elsa would sing, "Let It Go." Incidentally, this is a close cousin to the delegation change mentioned earlier.

It is my wish that every dentist would take a proactive approach to helping the millions of undiagnosed and untreated patients out there. Please do your part to save lives, heal relationships, and extend careers.

SECTION 2

FIG. 6 "COMMUNICATION"

NOBODY BUYING WHAT YOU'RE SELLING?

Which of these best describes you?

- You've taken some courses, watched a few webinars, subscribed to the trade rags, and then ... nothing.

- You're treating 2–22 patients per month, but you've plateaued.

- You've been working in sleep medicine for a long time. You give lectures, you keep up with new developments, you go to meetings, and everybody knows you—and yet most of your dental income is generated through restorative work because you still haven't really figured out how sleep fits into your practice.

None of these situations can be addressed with a better device, a novel sleep testing ring, a better billing service, or changes to PDAC requirements. What has the power to level the barriers and propel you to the next level? Did you guess new software? A new wearable sleep tracker? If so, please re-read the first part of this book, and pay attention this time.

The answer is (drum roll, please) *communication.* By mastering communication, you can obliterate self-imposed limitations and increase your sleep production. You're a skilled clinician and a successful businessperson. Why wouldn't you want to add "adroit communicator" to your toolkit? Look at other fields. Attorneys need to know the law, but they also need to be excellent communicators if they want to succeed.

Baseball managers have to know the game, but it's paramount they know what makes players tick so they can get the best performances out of them. The worst managers bounce from team to team until they end up in single

A ball as third base coaches. The best ones have charisma for innings and admirable communication skills. They earn fat salaries on coveted teams, eventually landing enviable broadcasting gigs. Communication sets them apart.

It's not that much different for you; becoming a strong communicator is another way to make yourself more dynamic and separate yourself from the pack.

IT'S JUST A COUPLE OF
NIGHT GUARDS, RIGHT?

"Some people want it to happen, some people wish it would happen, and others make it happen." —Michael Jordan

You're reading this because you want to grow DSM in your practice, right? You've attended CE courses that spent a lot of time fine-detailing the purportedly miraculous features of the sponsor's appliance while painting the rest of dental sleep medicine in abstract broad strokes.

The lecture was riveting. The speaker burrowed deep into the nitty-gritty details. Many dentists enjoy this level of product minutiae, and it makes sense. Crown margins are measured in microns. CBCT image quality is quantified in voxels, and setting times come down to seconds. OAT adjustment is a natural magnet, and DSM is laden with many other measurements that will fascinate the pedant in you. From home sleep test artifacts and cardiopulmonary coupling to the positive predictive value of BMI on treatment outcomes, there is a plentitude of opportunities to flex your analytical mind.

"Use our device because it can be titrated anteriorly in .02 mm increments and .1 mm vertically; 100 percent of patients experienced sleep while wearing the device."

Unfortunately, this myopic focus will not launch you into sleep medicine success. It might even stunt your growth. Most dentists who attend weekend courses wet the bed when it comes to implementation, or they fail to surpass more than two patients per month. The reasons have nothing to do with appliance selection, diagnostic validity of peripheral arterial tone, or other granularities you might focus on.

You hold the DSM magic wand. Choose whatever device you like. Select the best HST service and a billing company that gets you paid. But you don't need a magic wand to achieve this fantasy; there are a few good companies in every category. You can work with them, and you should, but I guarantee that you won't get far unless some other things change.

If you polled 100 dentists who treat more than 10 patients each month consistently, they'd tell you that their biggest challenges are:

1. Maintaining physician referral volume

2. Presenting treatment so patients move forward

3. Getting paid

4. Managing the team

These have none to do with titration mechanisms or tensile strength. The common thread running through those four challenges is communication. It's the antidote to what ails you. That's the focus of our next section.

Applying these tenets and improving conscientiously will result in more patients saying yes to treatment, higher testing rates, better team morale, and a happier home life.

A.D.I.D.A.S.
(ALL DAY I DREAM ABOUT
SELLING)

You're a salesperson. You might think, "I'm a doctor and a medical professional, a healer; I'm not selling anything!" On page one of his influential book, *To Sell Is Human*, Daniel Pink writes, "I spend a significant portion of my days trying to coax others to part with resources. Sure, sometimes I'm trying to tempt people to purchase books I've written. But most of what I do doesn't directly make a cash register ring."

Before you begin getting all self-righteous about your role as a clinician, not some lowly salesperson, know this: *everything* is sales. In *To Sell Is Human*, Pink remarks that, "Healthcare and education both revolve around non-sales selling: the ability to influence, to persuade, and to change behavior while striking a balance between what others want and what you can provide them. And the rising prominence of this dual sector is potentially transformative." In other words, selling healthcare saves lives. You're already doing it. The goal of this section is to help you do it more effectively.

People hate "sales." They despise "salespeople" with even greater fervor. That's why when a practice management consultant starts yammering about how to sell a case, your face contorts like they just offered you old eggs and tuna. It triggers the haughty British Royalty voice in your head that insists, "I do not sell. That is disgusting. I am a Doctor...."

Later, Pink recounts how Mike Cannon-Brookes, CEO and founder of Atlassian, a company that averaged $100 million per year in sales had no salespeople. Cannon-Brookes describes how prospective customers download a free version of the software. Then, if they're interested in the premium version, they call the company, and support staff "simply helps people understand the software, knowing that the value and elegance of their assistance can move wavering buyers to make a purchase." Sound familiar? You screen a patient or get a referral. Then you discuss their health concerns, learn more about them, demonstrate empathy, propose a solution, and deliver. That, my friend, is "sales."

Physicians engage in "sales" all the time. They help families make the decision to end life-support. Your hygienist explains to patients why smoking is bad and offers cessation resources. A person inspires another to accept their marriage proposal. You may not think of it as "selling," but all of these activities are in fact sales.

Your spouse emails links to several health spas in Fiji. They send you screenshots of the weather forecast there. Conversation turns to how long it's been since "we had a nice beach together to just relax." You are being sold.

You're going to relate to your patients' sleep issues, help them uncover the causes, and understand the negative impacts on their lives. You'll explain the full gamut of treatment solutions and highlight how you can help. Then you'll map out the process for them, answer questions, and provide exemplary patient care. Maybe this upends your notion of "sales," but if we can agree to redefine sales as "persuading or influencing someone to exchange resources with you," then we're ready to move forward.

FIG. 7 "FRONT TIRE"

RIDE THE BIKE

Developing sales skills is like riding a bike. There are two wheels, and in this analogy, the rear wheel represents your technical knowledge and clinical skills. The back wheel is supported by CE courses, webinars, textbooks, journals, and study clubs—standard stuff. You need this, and most dentists have pretty solid back wheels.

This is your wheelhouse (sorry, I couldn't resist). You live in a world of double-blind studies and peer-reviewed journals. You're probably intrigued by the various appliance types, their working mechanisms, and the different materials. You might even be interested in the pathophysiology of the apneic's airway, the artifacts seen in a sleep test's raw data, and figuring out the role of myofunctional therapy.

Sans a front wheel, you have a unicycle—difficult to maneuver, choose a direction, or get anywhere quickly. Your front wheel consists of your relationship and communication skills. These interpersonal relationship skills—what The 100 Club members focus on—are what most practices are lacking. This is where you have tremendous growth opportunities. Maintaining your front wheel is more difficult than the rear. The front wheel is going to guide you. It steers the conversation, and it empowers you to make the most out of your rear wheel.

If you cultivate and maintain your front-wheel skills, you'll get more patients to ebulliently move forward with treatment. It'll reduce tension in your practice, improve team engagement, and it will increase production and revenue.

These are my goals for you, dear reader. Let's get pumped.

STRANGER DANGER, SQUARE PEGS, AND EMPTY PROMISES

"The single biggest problem in communication is the illusion that it has taken place."
—*George Bernard Shaw*

Lately, when you're not working, you're ferrying kids from practice to rehearsal and dropping them off at sleepovers and play dates. All the kids. All the equipment. You decide it's time to acquire a new minivan, and you meet Pat, a salesperson at the car dealership.

"Hey, how are ya?", Pat asks mustering all the sincerity of *Kingpin's* Ernie McCracken.

Deja vu. Your mind goes to all the other Pats you've encountered. Whether it was a house, a minivan, or a new suit, "Pat" is on a mission to sell you something.

Buckle up. You're about to go for a ride through the four obstacles to selling.

THE FOUR OBSTACLES TO SELLING

Stranger Danger: Pat's appearance is disheveled: partially untucked polo shirt and three-day stubble that screams, "I'm going through a divorce!" He's smiling, but it feels forced and fake. Every syllable he utters gives you the heebie-jeebies, but you need a van.

People want to buy from capable sellers who they believe have their best interests in mind. We want to deal with people who look like we expect them to look, who are relatable, who share our interests, and who possess a sense of propriety that's appropriate to their position. So far, you don't really know Pat. Maybe your guard just automatically goes up when you're dealing with sales reps. It's normal to doubt whether Pat has your best interests at heart. He's a stranger to you, and he's a salesperson, for crying out loud.

This is how many patients feel when a dentist talks to them about SDB. "What are you trying to sell me now?" they wonder when their only interaction with you is a terse hygiene check. When they say, "Yeah, I go out to my car to take a nap on my lunch break and you respond with, "That's unsurprising as your ESS is 22. Your diurnal fatigue can be an indicator of SDB, quite likely UARS," there's a disconnect. You're not communicating on their level. They don't follow, and progress is practically nil.

Not My Problem: Back in the car showroom, Pat guides you to a two-seater Lamborghini. "It's sexy, and it's really, really fast." You tell him you're expecting triplets, but he just keeps going—horsepower this and speed that—apparently not giving a damn about you or your needs. He's trying to solve a problem that you don't have. Or maybe you do, but he's doing a lousy job helping you see it.

Pat didn't ask if you have kids. Nor did he inquire about your commute time, extracurricular activities, or pets. These are all probing questions that would reveal info that precludes you from being the ideal Lambo buyer.

How do you find out what your patients' problems are? What questions do you ask to identify their motives or uncover their chief complaints? People make buying decisions for a wide variety of reasons: financial gain, status, approval, and more. Different people give weight to different factors when they make decisions. If you want to sell to them properly, you'll need to identify their motives, their desired outcomes, and find out what else matters to them.

Rambling on about ESS scores, excessive pharyngeal tissue, and new OAT efficacy studies is the sleep dentist's version of what Pat just subjected you to. The patient in your chair might not be overly concerned about the health impacts of untreated OSA. They might not even care about the positive health outcomes that treatment might deliver. Maybe they just want to spend the night with their new love interest without the embarrassing snoring. Your intentions might be good, but if you're trying to solve a problem that isn't the one they want solved, you're not going to get anywhere with them. It cripples collaboration and murders momentum.

Square Peg: Pat won't stop pushing the Lamborghini. You tell him you need a vehicle that will carry four kids to the in-laws' while you're working, but he's already talking about the rebates you'll get if you buy before the end of the month.

"These babies become vintage real quick. You could probably sell it in ten years for twice what you pay today. Plus, the interior is genuine albino rhino." You couldn't care less. You aren't a "car person," and you're looking for a friggin' mini-van. This is the definition of the "square-peg-in-the-round-hole" idiom.

Everyone has problems, and everyone has potential solutions, but not every solution can solve every problem. To propose a workable solution, first you have to understand your counterpart's current situation, their desired situation, and what prevents them from bridging the gap.

You aren't playing tug-of-war. You're dancing. Only when you're both in step can you design a useful, mutually beneficial bridge. Otherwise, you're Pat. Don't be Pat.

Well-intentioned dentists often stroll into MD's offices extolling the superiority of oral appliances to PAP therapy when trying to establish a potential referral relationship.

"Doctor Shaddup, here's the deal: most of your patients don't wear their CPAPs. That's why we invented these oral appliances. Here's what a sample device looks like. Note that it's a milled device, titratable in less than 1 millimeter increments. The turnaround time is only five days, and it's adjustable with a simple acrylic bur. We'll take excellent care of your patients. We take medical insurance, we insist on efficacy studies, and we report on patient progress every step of the way. You should probably just send all your mild-to-moderates over to me. So, when you wanna start sending us your CPAP failures?"

Can you see how this might slam on the brakes in the selling process?

Empty Promises: Buyer's remorse rears its ugly head every time you get behind the wheel. Pat promised that you'd embody the chutzpah of Cardi B and the glamour of Christie Brinkley in the *Vacation* movies. Instead, you're looking into how to sell your kids on the dark Web so you can make the payments. Your spouse left you because of your questionable decision, and your new Lamborghini just sits in the driveway most of the time. Even though Pat said he'd throw in free oil changes for a year, by the time you actually needed one, it cost you $100. You told the mechanic what Pat said, but Pat's at lunch and they *never* do free oil changes. You are ready to go full-Michael-Douglas-in-*Falling-Down*-mode.

Earlier, I wrote that people want to buy from those who seem to have their best interests in mind. Let's bring it full circle. In the Pat scenario, you got pressured into buying something you didn't want, from someone you don't like, and now they've failed to deliver. To avoid doing this to others, we should be accountable and upfront. We should say what we'll do and then do what we say. When that doesn't happen, it leads patients to lose trust, and they experience cognitive dissonance. Then we're opening the door to lawsuits and negative reviews while pulverizing potential referrals and positive word-of-mouth advertising.

A few days after leaving Dr. Shaddup's office, you receive two referrals from him. You smirk and nod knowingly, "Damn, I must've really killed it with that presentation."

Of course, it couldn't have anything to do with your sleep champion going to lunch with Dr. Shaddup's office manager. Whatever. Brandie gets both patients appointed. What do you do? One patient balks because your fee is $4,500 and you only "assist" with filing the claim. The other patient moves forward and you deliver the device. However, the promised titration test fell through the cracks and never got done. Guess who's never referring another patient to you? You are your worst enemy and poor communication is your weapon of war.

Amidst your rage, it hits you like the final scene of *Usual Suspects* when Chazz Palminteri realizes Kevin Spacey is really Keyser Soze. That SOB, Pat. You've seen Pat in the mirror. Many times, in fact. If we're honest with ourselves, we probably play the role of Pat each time a patient declines treatment, an MD decides not to refer patients to you, or an employee refuses to do what's needed.

We don't bother taking the time to relate to the other person by building trust, expressing empathy, and demonstrating shared goals. We fail to explore their needs and their reality, and what's causing the chasm. Instead of asking questions and actively listening to their answers, we recommend solutions that might not address their unique situation. We push *our* solutions instead of the solutions that make the most sense for them. Finally, we move on to the next patient, problem, or task without delivering the support and follow-up we promised when we were selling our solution.

Let's look at how these four obstacles manifest in Dr. Dumass's sleep practice.

Stranger Danger: Dr. Dumass walks in for a hygiene check.

"Hi, I'm Dr. Dumass. It's nice to meet you. Everything looks good with your teeth. You've been doing a good job." At this point he chuckles because he mistakes his surface banter for humor and connection. He continues, "I noticed that you have a large neck, and you have scalloping on your tongue. Have you ever been treated for sleep apnea?"

You were already a little uncomfortable because you're at the dentist's office, interacting with an authority with whom you have little previous experience. He mistakenly implied this is the first time you've met, and then he told you out of the blue that you have a fat neck.

Not My Problem: Dr. Dumass continues, "Sleep apnea is really bad. You could die in your sleep if you don't take care of this. Don't you want to be able to play with your kids? We make oral appliances that treat sleep apnea."

With a furrowed brow, you glance over at Dr. Dumass's computer screen. You definitely included information about your CPAP use in your new patient paperwork. Why isn't it on the screen? Last time you were here you told Dumass that your whole family left you after you foolishly bought a Lambo.

When he removes the explorer from your mouth for the final time, he starts again, "It's often called the 'silent killer.' A lot of people don't even realize they have it."

Annoyed but polite, you chime in, "I've been diagnosed with sleep apnea, and I don't think I could sleep without my CPAP. I'm finding that I can live without my kids though after they left with my husband. Like I told you last time."

Nonplussed, he responds in Dumass fashion, "Yeah, it's really bad, and most people hate their CPAPs. Did Regan talk to you about our appliances? We treat sleep apnea, and you'll really like this appliance because it's easy to wear and most people won't even wear their CPAPs. Kids are really great. Bummer to hear."

Dr. Dumass was really focused on solving a problem. It just wasn't your problem.

Square Peg: Dr. Dumass didn't stop there. "It's much smaller they are than a CPAP, and insurance covers the treatment, too. You can see how much sexier an appliance is compared to that CPAP. I mean, who wants to wear that anyway? Right? Right?"

Dumass didn't ask you any meaningful questions, and he didn't really listen when you explicitly shared relevant details with him. You have severe OSA. You love your CPAP. You're considering INSPIRE therapy. He just hammered away with his OAT solution without concern for *your* concern.

Empty promises: Despite your repeated declinations, he relentlessly rebounds like Rowdy Roddy Piper in *They Live*'s epic six minute fight scene.

"Don't you want an appliance as a backup in case the power goes out? What about when you're camping? Shouldn't you have one just in case?"

Some of this actually makes sense. Plus, you wanted to shut him up, and he assured you that your insurance would cover all but $200 of it. And you booked a five-day Monument Valley glamping trip in an attempt to win your family back. That storm last March knocked out your power for three days, too. So, you agree to move forward. They take impressions, you provide a credit card, and about a month later, when you go back for your device, it falls off your teeth, *and* they have the audacity to bill you $2,800 because they didn't realize your deductible reset.

RELATE · EXPLORE · ADVISE · DELIVER

FIG. 8 "READ"

R.E.A.D. THE ROOM

I first learned about a codified consultative selling process two decades ago, in Wilson Learning's *Win-Win Selling*. Many of the concepts in this section are based on that work, and also on the works of Seth Godin, Dale Carnegie, Lawrence Zenk, Jeffrey Gitomer, Adam Grant, Chris Voss, Dr. Mark Murphy, and *Harvard Business Review*. The symbiosis of their works has served my career well, and I am forever indebted to them, along with all the other mentors who have guided me. By sharing their ideas with you, I'm paying it forward as others did for me. I hope you will do the same. Through giving, we receive.

In my experience and that of others I've coached, this process is indispensable. You should incorporate it into every area of your life. It will make you a better communicator, a more confident leader, and a better dentist, parent, partner, and friend.

DSM is rife with acronyms, and it's time to introduce a new one to represent this proven process. There is no debate or controversy as to its efficacy, like there is with AHI or STOP-BANG. This acronym and the process it represents are irrefutably effective, period. Full stop (bang).

You've heard someone say you should "read someone's body language" or "read the room." Let's consider how to READ your customer.

When following this process, you must follow the steps in order:

Relate: People prefer to do business with those they believe have their best interests in mind. If they relate to you, trust you, and feel comfortable with you, they are more likely to open up and share their needs and goals with you. This level of trust, candor, and vulnerability opens the doors to further exploration.

Explore: Patients know what their problems are, what keeps them up at night. They know what they want their future to be like, and yet they don't always know what they need to do to achieve it. Explore their needs and goals, ask the right questions, and actively listen—these steps can help you help them, and by helping them, you're helping yourself.

Advise: Only after relating to build trust and exploring to understand the person's problems and ambitions, can you recommend a solution. This solution probably won't be the canned speech you prepared about how, "The mandible is repositioned during sleep to maintain a patent airway, blah, blah, blah ..." It will be a co-created solution between you and your patient.

Deliver: If performed properly, the steps taken up to this point will deliver the ever-elusive, but oft-sought win-win solution. There will be no buyer's remorse, requests for refunds, or nebulous legal threats. You say what you'll do and do what you say. This will lead to five-star Google reviews, more patient referrals, and a sense of purpose that infuses every area of your life.

When meeting a new patient, referral source, or general contractor, we're starting at a high level; we're 30,000 feet up. As we move through the process outlined in the following section, we gradually bring this baby down for a successful landing together. Descending too rapidly can cause vomit bags to come out and unnecessary turbulence for everyone. Hell, you can bring it straight down if you want to, nosediving into a terrific crash and burn. That's what happens when we act like Pat.

You can also spend too much time and overshoot the runway, forcing you to loop back around. This is what happens when we educate endlessly without connecting the dots and advising our counterparts what to do next. Unfortunately, sometimes we run out of fuel or get redirected. This results in patients deciding to "think about it."

Let's fly high, and then descend smoothly for a comfortable landing as we highlight how these processes apply to your life and lay out some real-world examples that you can use today. Roger?

FIG. 9 "RELATE"

RELATE

"When you show deep empathy toward others, their defensive energy goes down, and positive energy replaces it. That's when you can get more creative in solving problems."
—Steven Covey

Relating is the first step to creating common ground and building trust. Don't believe me? Car salespeople have the worst reputations. Remember Pat? They're seen as smarmy, disingenuous, and untrustworthy. It doesn't have to be that way, though. Once I was in the market for a car and bought one from a particular sales rep solely because he did such an incredible job relating. He commented on the *Shelter* shirt I was wearing and mentioned his familiarity with the band. By the time I signed the paperwork, I realized I was doing it as much (maybe more) to make my "new friend happy" as to satisfy my need for a new car. Since then, I've referred several other people to him. We want to do business with people we like and who remind us of ourselves.

Thanks to traffic, you started the day a few minutes late. Of course, you're busy and stressed, and time is a scarce resource. This is not unique to dentists, of course; it's the same for any human being living in the 21st century.

In these harried times, one of the first casualties is empathy—relating to the plight of another. When you ask questions like, *"How are you doing today?"* the typical response is, "Fine, and you?" It's a common courtesy, nothing more. If they told you how they're actually doing, you'd really be behind and then you'd probably complain about it to everyone who will listen.

"Rainy day out there, huh?" Are you a freaking meteorologist on Channel 5? Or are you considering pitching this dentistry thing and focusing your career on becoming Captain Obvious full-time?

Small talk is fine, but a robocaller or ChatGPT can do that better than you can. Quit being an asocial weirdo, buzzing from op to op like a Tasmanian devil. Empathize with the human in front of you. Building real connections doesn't have to monopolize your time. Update the patient notes with any personal matters you pick up on. If they're wearing a 5k shirt, ask how they did in the race. If they have on a Cincinnati Bengals hat, ask if that's their team.

Pay attention to cues that give you important information—vital details about who your patient is beyond "36 y/o male." Afterward, have someone—an assistant, yourself, or a dictation app—add this information to the patient's chart. Next time they come into the office, take 10 seconds to review the patient notes. Then stroll into the operatory and start with, "Run any races lately?" or "How're the Bengals' doing?" These are simple steps that go a long way to reduce personal pressure.

Be sure you're asking the right people the right questions though. Ask the runner about the Bengals, and you'll increase personal pressure, erode trust, and create an awkward situation. It'll make you seem shifty, and people won't want to work with you.

You're a smart puppy with a brain like a steel trap, right? You remember everything, right? Um, you have 1000 patients. Take notes!

PRESSURE BAD, FRICTION GOOD

Stranger Danger is real. It's fomented by the miscalibration of friction and pressure. Friction and pressure typically have negative connotations. *Webster's* defines friction as, "... resistance to motion between bodies in contact ..." The definition for pressure doesn't feel much better. It's partially defined as "the stress or urgency of matters demanding attention." Pressure and friction conjure thoughts of litigious patients or overdue student loans.

High pressure can lead you to make rash decisions. Pressure can drive you to lose your temper, blow up at your family, or be curt with team members and patients. If you're over-leveraged, over-committed, or simply over it, pressure can boil over. Most of the time, you want to reduce pressure. Reducing pressure can help you relax or turn you into a veritable god when you get a patient out of pain. We just have to know how to apply the right pressure at the right time.

Personal pressure is high when your prospect doesn't know you or your intentions. We've evolved to evaluate outsiders as potential threats while looking for similarities. In his seminal book *Influence,* psychologist Robert Cialdini writes, "We like people who are similar to us. This fact seems to hold true whether the similarity is in the area of opinions, personality traits, background, or lifestyle." Neither Professor Cialdini nor I are advocating for homogeneity at work or anywhere else; we're merely acknowledging that, generally, like is attracted to like. Yankees fans like to be around other Yankees fans. Foodies enjoy the company of other foodies. And I'd prefer not to hang out with any of those people.

To move any relationship in the desired direction, it is paramount that we reduce personal pressure. We can do this by allaying concerns, demonstrating commonality, and proving our shared aims. Doing this over time decreases pressure, the relationship improves, and people are more comfortable with us. They're more open to our message and our intentions. They lower their guard. They may even be eager to hear what we have to say.

Friction can impede progress in your DSM practice. If you're using a third-party HST company that doesn't contact your patient promptly, it'll cause friction with the patient. Running a sleep marketing campaign and not scripting how to address calls with your team can lead to unwanted friction when the phones ring. Then your conversion rate plummets, and you'll have friction with your marketing partner.

Functional friction turns seemingly negative friction into a positive. This occurs when you and your prospect desire a similar outcome, and you lead them down the road to salvation. Your patient is tired of being tired and, based on their HST results, you can likely help: a WIN-WIN scenario.

Many sleep docs increased referrals to dentists during the 2021 PAP recall. Their patients couldn't get PAP devices, but they still needed treatment. Dentists who previously took steps to reduce personal pressure with their medical colleagues saw steep increases in referrals from those docs.

During the initial stages of a prospective business relationship, the prospect or patient may not be particularly motivated to keep things moving with you because they don't know you or trust you enough yet. It's your job to lower the personal pressure while ratcheting up the functional friction. Reduce the personal pressure by relating, highlighting similarities, looking the part, and using mirroring language. Increase functional friction by clearly demonstrating your intent to move forward in a mutually beneficial manner.

Once you've properly calibrated the personal pressure and functional friction gauges, the world is your oyster. People will trust you, and they'll be eager to open up to you.

BUILD TRUST

Your mom didn't fully trust your dad during their first date. The bank didn't give you a loan to start your practice without an interview and credit check. Similarly, your new patient is not going to trust you to treat their OSA, a serious medical condition, when they show up for their $49 Groupon cleaning. Trust isn't inherited, and it shouldn't be taken for granted. It has to be earned, and the seeds of trust must be cultivated before you can reap the harvest.

This process needn't take a long time, and there are actions you can take to expedite the pace. If you go too fast, though, it can have a deleterious effect and elongate the timeline. Worst case, it might even halt progress. There are some telltale signs when a patient doesn't trust you. They may look at their phone while you're talking. They may interrupt you to ask unrelated questions. They might avoid eye contact or exhibit closed body language cues such as crossed arms or anxious foot tapping.

The onus is on you to change the course by increasing functional friction and decreasing personal pressure. We achieve this by highlighting similarities, demonstrating competency, and displaying motivation. It ain't that tough, yo.

FIND COMMON GROUND

At the time of this writing, a heated cultural debate is raging about the scourge of homogeneity and the benefits of diversity. Despite what people say in public, however, most of us want to work with people who sound like us, who hold similar beliefs, and have comparable backgrounds. These similarities make us feel comfortable and secure, and these feelings can translate to trust.

This is a generalization, of course, but a litany of research supports the idea. It doesn't mean you should disregard your authentic self or play a character, but there are always opportunities to seek commonality. You might start with, "Hey, we're both wearing red shoes. We're red shoe twinners!" Assuming you're both wearing red shoes, that is.

Look for similar interests, common backgrounds, and shared contacts. Do you own the same handbag? Have kids the same age? Listen for clues about where they grew up or where their family lives. Share your own connections to those areas. Find out what kind of car they drive or how many kids they have or what sports teams they follow. These can all strengthen new bonds and go a long way to cultivating trust.

Mirroring language is an excellent way to accentuate similarities. If your patient says, "At the end of the day, I just want to sleep through the night and not be tired all morning," then you can naturally mimic that phrasing. For example, "Stacey, we're going to do everything we can to help you sleep through the night, so you're not exhausted all day." It isn't rocket surgery. Like Rob Schneider's character says in *Waterboy*, "You can do it!"

LOOK THE PART

You made dinner reservations for your anniversary: white linen tablecloths, five stars on Yelp, a $90 scallop appetizer that wouldn't feed a scallop, and a wine list doesn't feature prices. Then your server appears, wearing Crocs and a Motley Crue t-shirt. He's polite and knowledgeable about the wine list, but it's difficult to ignore his exotic attire. It clashes with your expectations for this otherwise ritzy environment.

As a medico-dental professional, looking the part boosts your credibility. There's no specific dress code. It might mean scrubs, or it might include a golf shirt, slacks, and a lab coat. I'm writing this in a pair of running shorts and a Run The Jewels t-shirt because I'm a writer at home. When I meet with dentists, I rock a suit and tie or jacket and a collared shirt at minimum.

Every time. You only get one chance to make a good first impression. This is important for meeting with potential physician referral sources, too. Dress professionally. Don't wear a ball gown or tux. That's inappropriately formal. Don't wear jorts and a tank top. That's inappropriately informal. Just dress for the occasion. Business casual is suitable for most situations.

Think about the restaurant with the heavy metal server. The entryway, the host who greeted you, the music, the decor ... It's all part of selling you that $90 appetizer and $300 tomahawk steak. This is part of the propriety smackdown. What image does your practice present? What does your waiting area look like? How does your front desk concierge greet patients? What's hanging on your walls?

You don't have to go broke outfitting your office. One of the top practices in the country decorated its waiting room with my old living room furniture. It looked nice, but we wanted new stuff. Go creative, not broke.

There are other simple steps you can take to improve perceptions. Frame certificates and articles you've written. Display awards you've earned and photos with prominent figures. Without looking like a self-centered blowhard, you can craftily reference achievements. "Hey, are you a Cardinals fan? I noticed your T-shirt. I was their team dentist for a few years."

Now that you're relating like a pro, it's time to ask the MD to refer all their patients over to you, right? Not so fast, you don't want to prematurely articulate. First, you need to explore.

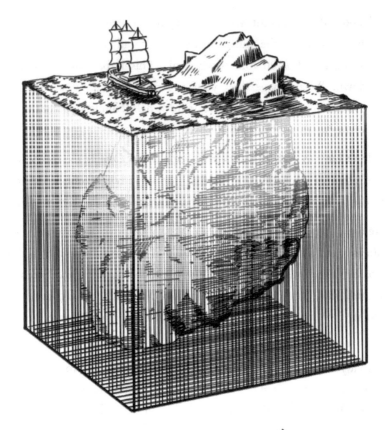

FIG.10 "EXPLORE"

EXPLORE

"A prudent question is one-half of wisdom." —Francis Bacon

How different would life be if Pat asked you some questions to understand your transportation needs? You'd still be married with kids and a reasonable car payment. Anyway, you're at the office. Time to focus. You've reduced personal pressure with your patient, and you're chatting about your shared alma mater. What's your next step?

Explore. Ask questions. People love to talk about themselves. Discover. This is what you think you're doing when you ask, "Still sunny out there?" or "Anything changed since the last time you were here?" What do you want to know? The patient might be overly chatty, but you have the power. You can always shut them up with a Columbia or your mirror.

Patients are icebergs. They come in for a prophy, but much more lies beneath the surface. Exploring can uncover more opportunities. This is also true of employees and most other people you'll encounter. That hygienist might be tired of scaling and root planing. Have you asked her to rate her career satisfaction or where she sees herself in three years? Every customer— and remember, everyone is your customer—is different, but they often have categorizable similarities. If we simply accept what we see, we're probably shortchanging them.

Let's get back to your patient, a 65-year-old male new patient hygiene check. You've been chatting for a couple minutes. You were at the same college at the same time *and* your kids are both seniors at the same school. You're gellin'. You're relating like a pro. You note flat cusp tips. His chart says he's taking Sectral for HBP and uses a CPAP. Bingo.

Handing him the white nylon sample appliance from the shelf, you confidently offer, "Chuck, we treat sleep apnea here with oral appliance therapy. Here, take a look at this." You elucidate how the device protrudes the mandible and maintains an open airway.

Climaxing with several stats about OAT's efficacy, which you've dutifully committed to memory, the patient interjects with, "Doc, I've tried two of those, and my last dentist and my sleep doc all agreed that my sleep score thing of 102 means I gotta wear the mask. I wish I could wear one of these instead, but I gotta tell you, my CPACK has been a lifesaver. Why is every dentist trying to push this sleep crap now, anyway?"

Remember when Dr. Dumass smothered you with his OSA suspicions? How did you feel when he was pushing OAT down your throat without asking about your PAP? What would've changed if he had asked questions? We often default to problem-solver mode and try to skip this essential step, which can actually stunt, if not completely halt, progress. It's like seeing the tip of the iceberg and ordering, "full steam ahead" without any consideration for the massive body of ice lurking just beneath the water, waiting to gut your hull.

Exploring, discovery, gap analysis—whatever you want to call it, the goal is the same; we want to uncover our prospect's current state of being and their desired state of being, and identify what separates the two. Just ask them how they're sleeping, how they want to be sleeping, and what stands in the way. Sounds easy enough, right?

Unfortunately, in most instances, this approach will elicit useless feedback. People aren't very good at identifying their goals or their problems, but they're keenly aware of what their needs are. They know what keeps them up at night and stresses them out while they're at work. We need to ask questions to understand what those things are and help isolate the issues so they can see them, too. My job is to help you to explore your prospect's needs and uncover what lies beneath the surface.

I possess two skills: One is a practiced ability to ask questions that encourage others to reflect and share openly. I put this skill to use as a podcast co-host. I have also coached practices, customer service teams, medical billing departments, and a hodgepodge of others on how to internalize these teachings and harness the power of the exploratory process. In the following pages, I'll enumerate types of questions that have worked for others. Then we'll tie it together so you can make like Lewis and Clark and get your explore on. We live in a commoditized society. Exploring can set you apart and open up new frontiers.

NO GAP EXCEPTIONS

A gap analysis is the most direct path to understand where your prospect is, where they want to be, and what's separating the two. You'll ask targeted questions designed to reveal your prospect's pain points (current state); their goals, buying motives, and ambitions (desired state); and what chasms exist (the gap). You'll pose questions that lay bare the true problems, expose the real barriers and goals, and kick open the door to a better tomorrow. Here are some examples. Check it out and create your own...

How would you feel if your physician referrals tripled?

What would you do to make that happen?

How does your poor sleep affect your life?

If you stopped snoring, what would change in your life?

What is the number one issue your team faces?

What needs to happen to address the issue?

What would your ideal schedule look like?

What's standing in the way?

Why is that?

Why?

NON-BINARY IS THE WAY TO BE

SCENE 1

Me. Did you have a good day at school?

Brat. No.

Me. Why not?

Brat. Cuz it sucked.

THE END

Back to the lecture at hand, here's another example:

SCENE 2

You. Have you been wearing your appliance?

Dick. No.

You. Why haven't you been wearing it?

Dick. It's uncomfortable, and I usually forget.

THE END

Both of the kickoff questions in the two scenes above restricted the answers to binary responses: "yes" or "no." That's it. Think about how you've felt during these conversations: slight discomfort, possibly peeved. That's how Dick and Brat felt, too. Use open-ended questions when possible unless a binary response is what you need. "Have you been flossing" will be met with a "no" or a lie. Instead, ask "Why haven't you been flossing" or "How do you feel after you floss?" That's what you want to know. Ask that question. We'll come back to these examples later.

LIVIN' THE DREAM

"Hey, Karen, how's it going?"

"Oh, you know, livin' the dream."

There's 10 seconds you'll never get back. Gone, lost to the ether. This exchange didn't build rapport, nor did it lend any insight to why Karen is in your chair or what's caused her to stop wearing her device.

Remix that question and everything changes. "Karen, what's new and noteworthy since the last time we met?"

"Well, my daughter had my grandbaby. They finally had to induce her ten days after the due date. And, Doc, I was wearing that sleep thing, but it felt really tight on my front teeth. Plus, Sharon said I'm still snoring, so I just stopped wearing it."

With that question, you were able to relate to Karen as a fellow grandparent, *and* you learned that her device needs relief in the anterior and some additional titration.

"What's new or noteworthy in your week so far?"

I love that question because it's open-ended and, unlike "How's your day going?" it cannot be answered with an automatic, one-word response. They have to think, even if only for a second, before they reply. You're switching off their autopilot and bringing them into the moment.

What's next? This is where the beauty lies, and we hit the jackpot. Let's pose the same question to a couple other patients.

"What's new or noteworthy in your week so far?"

Terence shares, "I dropped my son off at baseball camp for the summer and my wife is visiting her family for a few weeks, so I'm living the bachelor life."

Christine responds, "I'm going to look for a new apartment because I want to get a second dog, and I need more space."

You're making human connections. Now you can joke with Terence about the bachelor life, ask about his son's baseball aspirations, or what he plans to do with that downtime. This helps you further build trust and provide priceless notes for the chart so you can reference it during Terence's next visit.

The same goes for Christine. "What kind of dog do you have now? What breed are you considering? How will you figure out whether they'll get along?"

Fortify human bonds. Your life will be enriched. Your patients will consider you to be worthy of their trust, and they'll say "yes" to more treatment and be more likely to follow your instructions. This isn't conjecture; it's fact. People buy from others they feel a bond with.

If you want to know more, first you need permission.

ASK FIRST, THEN ASK MORE QUESTIONS LATER

Always be building relationships. Be a nonstop relationship-building machine. Exploratory questions often yield useful information. However, before you go to second base, you'll need permission. It's a simple, yet often overlooked concept. Think of getting permission as a verbal contract to keep exploring.

"Congratulations, Karen! Boy or a girl?"

"A beautiful baby boy named Darren. I'd show you a picture, but my phone's in my purse."

"Be sure to show it to everyone at the front desk. Hey, do you mind if I ask you a few other questions about your snoring and where your device is tight?"

"No problem at all. Here, I'll show you where it hurts."

In this example, permission was granted readily. Still, permission questions are indispensable in the following patient conversation. . ..

"Steve, the form you filled out up front says that you snore and you're tired during the daytime. Do you mind if I ask you a couple questions about that?"

"I'm just tired all the time. My last girlfriend left me because I snored so loud. I'm going to a men's health clinic downtown for a consultation next week."

There's a positive correlation between how personal the info is that you're seeking and the importance of permission questions. Skip this step at your own peril.

THIN LINE BETWEEN LOVE AND HATE

Asking someone what they like most and least about a subject can help you decode what matters to them. Juxtaposing love/hate about something forces them to reflect and these questions will often elicit visceral responses. This is a particularly useful query to expose how a hiring candidate will react to negativity.

When interviewing new assistant candidates, ask them what they loved about the last office they worked at. Allow them to answer. Then ask what they hated. If they tell you they loved working just three days a week and denounce their former colleagues, keep that Indeed ad running for another week.

The next time you meet with a potential referral source, ask them to contrast what they liked about dentists they've worked with and what they wish had been different. "They always provided great communication about successfully treated OAT patients, but they kept mum about the ones whose AHI wasn't normalized." From this, you can extrapolate that the physician values transparent communication and is concerned about long-term patient care.

A MAGIC WAND IN A PERFECT WORLD

"Magic wand" questions encourage others to think big, beyond their real and imagined limits. Ask a doctor, "If you had a magic wand, what would your dream practice look like? How many days would you work? What would be your ideal patient volume? Income? Team size?"

Their responses can open doors to what makes them tick, their self-image, and their buying motives. For example, "Doctor, in a perfect world, what would your working relationship with a dentist look like?"

She might respond, "It's really important they communicate with me at every step. I need to know that the dentist will file the insurance and won't charge an obscene fee. I need to be confident that the patient gets the treatment they need so they don't leave me a nasty Google review. That's not going to work for me."

From this response, we can deduce that communication is important. We can also conclude that patient wellness is important, along with her practice's online reputation. Now that you're equipped with this magic wand, you can go out and help others create their perfect world.

CAN I GET YOUR NUMBER?

Assigning numeric values to things can help you narrow the focus. "Karen, during the three nights that you wore the device, on a scale of one-to-ten, how bad did it hurt with one being "no biggie" and ten being, "get me to the hospital now!"

If she rates it a two or a three, that's good; you can assure her that you'll relieve some of the pressure on the inside of the device and she's likely to notice a big improvement. If she gives it a six, you'll probably consider an NSAID along with a reminder that it commonly takes a week or so to acclimate to the new device. If she says it's a ten, you'll want to ask another permission question.

If paired with humor, your questions can build rapport while you uncover information. When interviewing a new front desk candidate, for example, you could say, "On a scale of one-to-ten, with one being my great grandma and ten being Bill Gates, how would you rate your ability to master a new software system?"

This will likely elicit a chuckle and help you understand your potential new hire's aptitude for implementing a new EMR.

THE FIVE WHYS

Driving your daughter to soccer in that Lambo procured from Pat's bitch-ass, she asks why her siblings didn't accompany you to practice. "They stayed back with your Uncle Chester."

"Why?" she innocently inquires.

White knuckling the wheel you reply, "Because we only have two seats in this car."

"Why?" your most prized cargo asks again.

"Because that's all Lamborghinis have seating for."

"Why" she asks, obviously confused.

Moonwalking the thin line between annoyed and pissed, you tell her that high-performance sports cars are made to go fast and impress others.

"Why?"

"Because I said so dammit and the salesperson manipulated me, and now your Dad and I are divorced, and your sisters are with your Uncle Chester and we're going to your soccer practice alone! DID YOU BRING YOUR SHIN GUARDS?"

Time to downshift…

The "five whys" concept lets you peel back multiple layers of problems and symptoms to expose the root cause. The method is deceptively simple; by asking "why" five times, you can get to the heart of the matter, putting you in a position to address the real issue.

Here's an example of how the five whys can be used in your sleep practice:

Your sleep assistant wants you to switch to IOS from analog impressions. Now's your time to shine. Ask for permission first. "Do you mind if I ask you a few questions first, so I'll understand what's up?"

"Sure."

"Why do we need to switch?" you ask.

"Because it's better for the patient," is her reply.

"Why is it better?"

"Because the way we do it now, they complain about impression material gagging them."

"I can see why that's an issue. Why is impression material going down their throats?"

"I dunno. I always follow the instructions on setting time, but the viscosity is still way off."

"Why do you think that's happening?"

"I don't know. I always follow the setting time, but I don't measure the amount of water exactly. I guess that might have something to do with it."

Maybe a scanner is a good investment. On the other hand, maybe measuring more carefully will do the trick. It's amazing how much info can be revealed through the five whys. Why?

Cuz I said so.

THINGS THAT MAKE YOU GO "HMMM"

You walk into a restaurant and the host greets you. "How's your evening going, Doctor?" he asks.

"Great, and you?"

"Wonderful, thank you for asking. Flora will show you to your table. Enjoy your meal."

"You, too, thanks," you respond absent-mindedly. He's not there to enjoy a meal. He's going to seat the next table. And so on.

We tend to fall into rote patterns in our conversations. Asking questions that make people think can help you engage them more fully. The principle still applies about not asking questions you don't want to know the answer to. You can have some real fun with this and be memorable to your patients.

I used to co-host a podcast. No one ever approaches me about topics we covered during the episodes. However, years later, people still joke with me about some of the questions I asked the guests.

"Do you like tapioca?"

"What's one thing you've gifted to several people?"

"What's the last amazing book you read?"

"When was the last time you got into a physical altercation?"

"What's a piece of conventional wisdom most people hold that you disagree with?"

"Do you believe in ghosts?"

Feel free to borrow some of these or go ahead and make up your own.

ONE AT A TIME

"If I wear this every night, can you give me a money-back guarantee that it'll work, and I'll be able to get off my high blood pressure meds and stop snoring? What if it only does one of these?"

Under that one umbrella question are multiple questions, requiring multiple answers. Can you guarantee that this will work? Will they be able to get off their meds? Can you promise they'll stop snoring? Will you give them their money back if it doesn't do some or all of these things? What will happen if it only achieves some of them?

You'll want to provide clear answers to these questions to avoid confusion later. "Pericles, I heard a few different questions in there, and I want to be sure you get all the answers you need. First, it sounds like you want to know if there's a money-back guarantee. I can't guarantee you that the device will eliminate your apnea. I can't guarantee it'll stop your snoring or get you off any meds. However, I can tell you that this method has worked for many other patients, and scads of research show that this treatment is very effective. However, every patient is different. I can guarantee we're going to do all we can to help you. We've helped a lot of people, and we want to help you, too. What other questions do you have?"

Don't subject other people to the multi-question barrage. Explore, with one thoughtful question at a time.

THEN SHUT UP!

At first, when flexing your new exploratory skills, you may feel one or more of the following compulsions:

- Pretend you're listening while you review your mental grocery list.

- Cut them off and tell them your solution to their problem.

- Yawn while wondering how they function in society.

- Provide active listening indicators such as "Mm-hm" and "I see," while not truly listening.

Here's the scoop. Don't ask if you don't want them to tell. Remember the iceberg analogy? Only the tip is visible, and you want to identify what's beneath the surface. Ask the questions, shut up, and listen. A wise man once counseled, "We have two ears and one mouth so that we can listen twice as much as we speak."

Humans speak an average of 130-words-per-minute, but our brains process speech at about five times that rate. It's your responsibility to slow the F down and give your prospects your full attention. This requires active listening.

You're busy, and you've bought into the myth that you're a fluid multitasker. You're not. It's distracting, and it makes people feel like commodities when you're buzzing about the operatory. You're not present. It's bad for you, bad for them, bad for business.

Ask questions. Make eye contact. It needn't linger for some weird length of time. Listen. Lean forward slightly. Don't cross your arms. Face them as much as possible. Selectively mimic their language. Nod affirmatively occasionally. Let them know that you're listening, you're present, and you're processing the information they're sharing with you. Relate. Explore some more.

"Yes, I've heard from other patients how hard it is to get used to their CPAPs. Fortunately, there are other options. What did your doctor tell you about oral appliance therapy?"

Don't look at your phone or your schedule. Lean in, look them in the eye, and listen.

IT WORKS
IF YOU WORK IT

There were a couple examples in the section on non-binary questions. Let's revisit those conversations and how different they sound when you apply the techniques you just read about.

SCENE 1 REDUX:

Me. What'd you learn in math class today?

Brat. We had a test, so that took up the whole class.

Me. What was on the test?

Brat. Adding and subtracting decimals.

Me. From 0.1 to 1.0, how do you think it went?

Brat: 0.7

Me. Why don't you think it's 0.9?

Brat. Because I didn't study enough.

Me. Why not?

Brat. Because I was too tired.

Me. Why?

Brat. I guess because I was playing *Call of Duty* on Twitch too late.

Me. If you had a time machine, what would you do differently?

Brat. I woulda studied one-third of the time, played my game one-third of the time, and gotten more sleep with the other one-third of the time.

Now let's apply our newfound exploratory skills to the OAT noncompliant patient from earlier.

SCENE 2 REDUX:

Me. You've been using your device for nearly two weeks now. How many nights have you been unable to wear it?

Dick. The first couple nights were pretty tough, but then I got used to it. Then it started bothering me again last night.

Me. Good, you're paying attention to what's bothering you. You mentioned that it was 'pretty tough' at first and that it 'started bothering you again last night.' Does that sound right?

Dick. Spot on, Doc.

Me. What was tough at first and what changed?

Dick. It was really tight on my upper front teeth, and it was hard to fall asleep. I'd take it out about 3:00 a.m. because it hurt. After a few nights, my wife told me to take a Bendadryl an hour before bed. After that, I slept with it in all night, but after a week of Bendadryl, I was like, 'I gotta stop taking these every night.' My wife is mad because she said I'd finally stopped snoring and she didn't have to stay up wondering if I was gonna die in my sleep.

Me. If we can get it comfortable for you, on a scale of 0 to 10, how likely are you to try wearing it every night again?

Dick. 10!

WHAT ELSE DID WE MISS?

These exploratory questions are examples that have worked for many others: Sales reps selling HST units to dentists and sleep champs selling OAT to patients. From parents helping their kids get on track with their grades to office managers negotiating performance reviews.

These are prompts, not a concrete script. Take them, smack 'em up, flip it, rub it down, and make them your own. It might feel awkward at first. The questions will sound unnatural as they leave your lips. That's OK. You're evolving. Continue to hone your questions as you identify what's working and what isn't.

If you want to accelerate your exploratory prowess, encourage your team to provide you with candid feedback about what's working and what isn't. Consider carefully what they share with you. Role playing typical scenarios with your team is a useful growth accelerator. It's better to fumble in practice situations than when it counts. You'll get better together and as individuals.

Daniel Pink's *To Sell Is Human* includes a poignant conversation with a high school teacher named Larry Ferlazzo. "It's about leading with my ears instead of my mouth ... It means trying to elicit from people what their goals are for themselves and having the flexibility to frame what we do in that context."

Now that we've related to our prospect and explored their wants, needs, and obstacles, the time has come to advise win-win solutions.

FIG. 11 "ADVISE"

ADVISE

"Approach each customer with the idea of helping him or her solve a problem or achieve a goal, not of selling a product or service." —Brian Tracy

Your patient is eating out of your hand. You bonded over yesterday's Bears game and your shared alma mater. Through exploratory questions, you discovered that he'd been diagnosed with mild OSA, tried PAP for three months, and refuses to wear it again. "It was impossible to fall asleep. I felt like a python was wrapped around my head, and I looked like a monster movie character. I ain't doin' it again."

The patient claims to feel fine, but he admits to being tired a lot, and he wants more energy so he can toss the ball with his son. Plus, he wants to placate his wife who's complaining about *her* lack of sleep. She calls it "the deathwatch" because she's worried that he's croaking in the middle of the night. Happy wife, happy life.

Everything you've done so far with this patient has led to this moment. You've established trust and demonstrated your desire to understand. It's time to offer your patient a solution.

Easy enough, right?

Well, yes and no. Most clinicians do a decent job recommending treatment. With a little refinement, all DSM practitioners can crush it though. In this section, I'll present simple steps that'll help you connect the dots for patients, so they naturally make the right decisions, bridging the gap between their current and desired states.

IT'S A FEATURE NOT A BENEFIT

Fanning them out like playing cards, you gesture to the array of devices on your desk, "Pick one, any one."

Your patient picks a Herbst. "This one's interesting," he says, holding it upside down and moving the telescoping rods back and forth.

"That's a Herbst," you say, "with a simplified titration mechanism and a uniquely user-friendly adjustment key. The metal framework is actually chrome. It's PDAC approved and while the company is in the U.S., their manufacturing hub is overseas."

"That's a mouthful", Terry snarks. He could have been talking about the acrylic and metal contraption or your overwrought description of it.

"That one next to it," you say, pointing to the dreamTAP, "was invented by Dr. Keith Thornton. He's a brilliant dentist who taught the first sleep course I ever attended. It's titratable in quarter millimeter increments. It only allows for anterior contact, so we'll probably want to add posterior stops for a tripod effect. Some people say it makes them feel claustrophobic because they're locked together, but I wore one for a few years and it was fine."

Pensive, the patient lets out a long, slow exhale. "You know, my wife is the one who has to sleep with me. Let me hold off today. I'll come back with her, and we can choose one together."

You hand him patient brochures from Dynaflex, ProSomnus, and Airway Management. "Sure, why don't you take these home and review them with your wife. Then give us a call when you're ready to get started."

Here's your mistake: You made it all about the features of the devices, instead of how the patient can benefit from those features, leading to a happier tomorrow. You needlessly regurgitated your DSM knowledge.

Advising properly means helping your prospect find the solution that works best for them.

That's the paradox of choice. Choices are great, but too many options can lead to anxiety, a sense of unease, and analysis paralysis. Think about it. Let's say you're having a date night with your partner. You don't know what you want, but you're starvin' like Marvin. They pick the Cheesecake Factory, where the menu gives you page after page of pastas and starters, followed by an appendix devoted to the restaurant's namesake. As you flip through this culinary *War and Peace*, your server stops by for the third time, "Are we ready to order yet?"

You feel bad asking *le garcon* to come back yet again, and so you nudge your spouse to order first. This sly tactic gives you an extra 17 more seconds to review your choices. You've narrowed it down to one of eleven entrees. The moment of truth has arrived. Panicking, you say, "I'll have the ribeye, medium rare, please," even though you're a vegetarian. Oh, well, you can always take it home for the dog.

Now safely in your DeLorean, you are hurtled back to the future flux capacitor style. What if you'd picked a different restaurant, one with a nice, well-designed, single-page menu with three salads, four appetizers, and a half dozen entrees, two of which are meatless?

Overloading your patient with options is a DSM practice's version of the Cheesecake Factory menu. Patients just want an easy solution to their problem. The consultation described above was way too heavy on features and jargon. The patient told you his mask felt like a snake wrapped around his head, and yet you introduced a device that gives some patients claustrophobia. Best leave that one out. Give them choices, but not too many. Narrow the choices to two or three options and briefly describe how their key features deliver significant benefits. You wouldn't just open the refrigerator and ask a four-year-old what they want for dinner, right? You ask if they want peas or carrots. More signal, less noise.

I'm going to share something that might sound contradictory to what I just described, but it can be a useful complement: Robert Cialdini's "contrast principle." The principle holds that we understand something better when we see it compared to something else. For example, you could juxtapose a bulky dual-arch dilator device with two devices that are appropriate for your patient. It's like the marketing concept so many dentists use when comparing a PAP mask to an oral appliance. Like Black Sheep said, "You can get with this, or you can get with that…"

You have to connect the features to the benefits. The patient and his wife want sleep, and the patient wants more energy. Don't act like a third-rate OAT sales rep four aisles removed from the main entryway at the AADSM annual conference.

Features are how something works. Benefits are why it matters. Unless your patient is a materials engineer, they're not going to care about the tensile strength of an appliance's PMMA trays. Nobody gives a damn about "titratable one-millimeter straps, color-coded for strength and flexibility."

Those features do matter, but only when you connect them to benefits. If you're still uncertain about how to distinguish a feature from a benefit, ask yourself, *so what?*

"This device comes with a five year warranty." *So what?* "So you know it's built to last and probably won't need to be replaced for a few years."

"This one is made from a super strong material." *So what?* "Looking at your teeth and your jaw muscles, I can see that you grind your teeth. This device will withstand all that grinding. It's the precision device I wear each night. Only the best for us, right?"

"The bands are easy to swap out, and they come in various different lengths and strengths." *So what?* "We can customize the device to your mouth, and if anything changes, we can swap out the straps quickly and easily. That way you won't have to get a new one prematurely. Good sleep is priceless, but it's not cheap."

Dentists often assume that patients who've been diagnosed and referred have been given thorough explanations about the cause of their sleep apnea, its impacts on their health, and available treatment options. However, an informal survey of patients at one DSM office revealed that more than 90 percent of patients were virtually uninformed as to their condition.

Read the room. Avoid the study club vernacular. Don't tell your patient that she has an Apnea Hypopnea Index of 27 and there were associated O2 desats with a nadir of 82 percent. Don't mention your concerns about this one piece of data, but it may just be an artifact. Bypass your mental flashcards related to the preponderance of evidence about the negative health implications of untreated OSA.

In *To Sell Is Human*, Daniel Pink shows readers the curse of knowledge, using Cathy Salit's "Conversation with a Time Traveler" improvisation exercise. Ms. Salit instructs us to gather a small group of people and pair them up. One person in each pairing should think of something that didn't exist 300 years ago, and then try to explain the item to the other person, who will pretend to be from the early 1700s.

From the book, "… to explain, say, a Big Mac, bought from a drive-through window, requires understanding a variety of underlying concepts: owning an automobile, consuming what three hundred years ago was a preposterous amount of meat, trusting someone you've likely never met and will never see again…" If we aren't careful, we fall victim to the curse of knowledge, and those we communicate with suffer the consequences.

Think about how you've felt in some Embassy Suites conference room for a CE course after the lecturer spent two hours on the first slide inundating you with their credentials and the following six hours inculcating you with information seemingly intended to make you think that he, and he alone, is the only person who can operate a successful sleep practice. This information isn't transmitted to you in a way that's digestible or actionable. That sucks. Don't do it to others.

Remember your favorite dental school instructors and most resonant DSM lecturers? They conveyed complex concepts in simple, relatable terms. Jazz musician Charles Mingus once said, "Making the simple complicated is commonplace. Making the complicated simple, awesomely simple, that's creativity."

The "Feynman Technique" can help transform you into one of those memorable folks. Richard Feynman, renowned theoretical physicist and winner of the Nobel Prize, developed a simple technique that can guide us to better patient communication and mastery of any topic.

There are four simple steps that can benefit you and all those you interact with:

1. **Pick a concept you want to know more about and learn about it.** Look for books, videos, and articles on the subject.

2. **Teach it to someone else:** a team member, a patient, a spouse, whomever. Simplify it like you're explaining it to a ten year-old. Anyone can complicate an explanation. Distilling it to the barest essence takes true understanding.

3. **Bridge the knowledge gaps.** What are the blind spots? Where do you get hung up? Learn more about those areas to bolster your understanding.

4. **Review and simplify further.** Try explaining it again. In our case, ideally you can explain clearly and concisely how OAT works, or any other topic, in a way that's easy to understand.

Consider this example from a sleep coordinator explaining test results in understandable terms. "Ms. Jackson, it looks like you stop breathing 27 times per hour while you're asleep. During that time, your brain isn't getting the oxygen it needs; your heart is racing because your body is suffocating. This happens over and over again, all night long."

Then she pauses to connect the dots and answer the unspoken *"so what?"*

The sleep coordinator continues: "When your heart is racing like this, 27 times per hour, more than 200 times per night, it's overworking all night, leading to a 140 percent increased risk of heart attack and double the risk of stroke. Each time you stop breathing, your brain forces you to wake up, not all the way, but enough. That's why you're tired all the time. I'm sure you can see how important it is that we do everything we can to take care of this, Ms. Jackson."

Note how the sleep coordinator artfully explained a complex and serious health matter in plain language, emphasized how dangerous it can be, cited a couple meaningful statistics, and closed by tying it to the patient's chief complaint: excessive sleepiness during the day. Finally, the sleep coordinator drove home the fact that they can likely help her.

That's how you advise like a pro. You can flaunt your encyclopedic OAT knowledge at conferences, but you need a whole different style when advising a patient. Limit the options to around three viable solutions and then tie the features to impactful benefits. Then …

ABC

We asked, *So what?*

Time to ask, *Now what?*

You're not doing this for your health; you're doing it for theirs. This exchange of information is all for naught if we don't prompt them to take action after you explain their options. The concept of closing gets a bad rap because of Alec Baldwin's high-pressure chiding of his service sales force in *Glengarry Glenn Ross*. ABC = always be closing. This is the Pat school of sales.

Don't do it. Instead, give your patient an off-ramp to make the sensible decision. "Which device would you like to take impressions for today?"

Give your physician counterpart an off-ramp by asking how she'd like you to refer patients and who on her end should receive your referral forms so she can do the same for you.

Actively listen and stay attuned to nonverbal cues. If you sense reluctance, it's not the end of the world. Say, "It's important for you to have all the information you need. What questions do you have?" Listen and give active feedback ("So what I hear you saying is …"). Clarify their questions and address their lingering concerns. Speak with accuracy and precision. Avoid nebulous phrasing and over-promising.

Reminder: avoid technical jargon and non-essential information. I hate it when an HVAC tech comes to my house and rattles off the technical engineering handbook for my air conditioner because I have no idea what he's talking about. Plumbers, too. I'm not a plumber. I don't want to be a plumber. I called the plumber because he's a plumber and knows about plumbing. I don't want a plumbing tutorial. If I have a rusted pipe that finally broke and started flooding my bathroom, don't explain the four different types of washers I should consider. The flooding is my problem, and the faulty pipe is the culprit. Show me the off-ramp and I'll show you the money. Tell me what needs to be done to fix it and how much it costs. You fix, I pay. Problem solved.

WORDS MATTER

"There are always three speeches for every one you actually gave. The one you practiced, the one you gave, and the one you wish you gave." —Dale Carnegie

I once worked for a software startup. At the beginning, the team was small, and everyone wore multiple hats. The lead developer was also the HR manager and the IT department. As the firm grew, our talent needs changed. We needed increasingly specialized knowledge and skill sets. A dental assistant who took a graphic design class wasn't going to cut it as we set out to build a more robust marketing engine.

As we sought to attract highly qualified candidates with relevant experience, we needed to provide a benefits package to make our openings more appealing. Offering a 401(k) plan was the first step. In the all-hands-on-deck startup spirit, the owner of the company worked to identify the best plan administrator for our needs. Our existing team would reap the benefits, and we'd be more appealing to prospective employees.

Unfortunately, when it came time to deliver this exciting information to the team, the owner made a grave communication faux pas. She kicked off the meeting with a soliloquy about how much time it took her to vet the various companies and how much it set back her other projects. She stressed that it strained her to do this, and it was a huge hassle.

After 15 minutes of bleating, she announced that everyone would receive an email with instructions for opting in if they chose to. She capped it all off with, "If we hit our goals this year and there's any money left over, the company will match up to 4 percent of your contribution, but I don't know if we're going to be able to. We'll have to see how the year goes. Any questions?"

Guess how many people signed up? Three: me, one other team member, and the owner's spouse. None of the other 10 people in the room that day chose to participate. They felt guilty. It seemed like they'd upset their boss even more if they joined.

In our post-meeting debrief, the owner lamented, "See, this was a big waste of time. Nobody even wants to do it." Cautiously, I suggested that the team was probably unfamiliar with compounding interest, employer matches, and what it all means for their paychecks and their futures. "How 'bout if we use the approaching deadline as a reason to revisit the topic during our next team meeting?" She agreed.

During the next meeting, we told a story. The narrative involved benchmarks we'd met in the previous year. We highlighted our growth and future goals and talked about how satisfying it was to offer the 401(k). We put a compounding interest calculator up on the monitor and toyed with different contribution amounts over years. The team's collective jaws dropped. They were amazed that such small amounts of pre-tax earnings could yield that much money down the road.

This time, all but one person opted in. We were proud to offer the benefit, and they were happy to work for a company that would do this for them. It's not just the message; it's the story and how it's communicated. Words matter. Tone matters. Communication matters. This is what sales is all about.

FIG. 12 "DELIVER"

DELIVER

"I'll tell you what I'm gon' do, and I'm'a do it, too." —*Froggy Fresh*

Despite Pat's previous promises of free oil changes, you still had to pay for them, and Pat was nowhere to be found. That's buyer's remorse. Big time. Similarly, you don't want to purchase new DSM software and get weak training and support afterward. You don't want to deliver two ill-fitting devices in one day and have the lab give you the cold shoulder. You want reliable support after the sale. You want to know that your vendor partners have your back and will make things right if they screw up. Your patients, referral sources, and others in your orbit deserve the same.

Simply stated, say what you'll do and do what you say. If you tell the patient that the home sleep testing company will contact them tomorrow, you'd better be confident that your HST service partner will call them tomorrow. If you schedule the patient's delivery two weeks out, you'd better work with a lab that doesn't doink around with turnaround times.

Set realistic expectations consistently by saying what you'll do and fulfill the promise by doing what you committed to. Every time. This builds trust, which, like interest, compounds over time. This is true of your team, too. They need to abide by these principles and practice them in all their affairs. This is how you create raving fans.

Otherwise, buyer's remorse rears its ugly head, and this also compounds. Every slipup or missed expectation—each molehill, no matter how inconsequential—becomes a mountain, a big mountain that could have been avoided.

SMALL EXPECTATIONS, BIG RESULTS

When I was a kid, I saved my allowance, and I used my savings to order items advertised on the backs of comic books. The pictures of seahorses looked unlike anything I'd ever seen, like aquatic equestrian aliens.

Three weeks later, the envelope arrived. With something approaching Christmas-morning-level excitement, I carefully opened the envelope. Can you say "disappointment"? The contents didn't look like they were from 20,000 leagues under the sea, more like the dust on my bookshelf. The ad depicted creatures that my GI Joe figures could ride around in the sink. In reality, if I carefully tended to the envelope's contents for a two months, there was a remote possibility that I might see something vaguely resembling the seahorses in the ad.

At some point, we've all been hexed by the curse of high expectations. You can safeguard against this with your patients by under-promising and over-delivering consistently. Do you promise patients that appliance therapy will work for them? When they ask if it's guaranteed to work, use understandable terms to explain the research, describe potential side-effects, highlight the lack of guarantee, and outline the options. Eliminate surprises and unrealistic expectations.

More recently, I had surgery. The surgeon assured me I'd be running again in three weeks. Six weeks later, I could barely walk and was experiencing severe pain. I demanded a follow-up appointment. While there, I was unable to get onto the exam table. Unconcerned with my state, the surgeon told me that three weeks is the typical recovery period but for many people it takes up to six months. That new information led me to reframe my progress and outlook. If he would have set this expectation from the beginning, I wouldn't have been in such a panic.

Tell your patients exactly what you'll do and then do it. "There's a library's worth of research to show that oral appliances work for the majority of patients and that nearly all patients prefer the comfort of an appliance to CPAP. There are some potential side-effects, most of which are minor, such as slight tooth movement and dry mouth. We'll review all of them with you and make sure you understand them. You've tried CPAP, so you're familiar with that. Other possible treatment options include some surgical interventions and lifestyle choices."

You're not finished yet. "Today, we'll take scans of your teeth and your jaw in different positions. It'll take about ten minutes. Then we'll send them to the lab so your device can be custom made. We'll schedule your appointment three weeks from now. I can't guarantee it'll work for you, but based on all the research and the patients I've seen, there's a strong likelihood that it will. I can guarantee that we'll do all we can to work with you to make your treatment a success."

IT'S ALL YOUR FAULT

DSM isn't complicated, but it can be complex. There are lots of moving parts and manifold variables. You mitigate them as much as possible, and yet issues can still pop up, whack-a-mole style. The doctor wants to know why he wasn't informed that his brother-in-law decided not to move forward. Apparently, your office didn't send a follow-up letter.

Let's pretend this is one of those OG *Choose Your Own Adventure* books. Do you:

1. Contact the doctor, throw your employee under the bus, and complain about the dearth of "decent help" these days?

2. Pretend nothing happened because you're conflict averse but berate your employee for the next week?

3. Reach out to the doctor and apologize for the oversight and remind him that you have systems in place to prevent this? Then inform him that you've reviewed the protocols with your team, identified

what went wrong, and you're pretty confident it won't happen again. Finally, you'll want to review the reasons why the brother-in-law opted not to move forward.

You probably chose option 3, but most people would actually *do* one of the first two. If you throw your employee under the bus, you'll look petty and disingenuous. If you choose option two, your employee is deprived of the opportunity to take corrective action. You'll also shatter your team's trust. They'll wonder what you say about them when they screw up. Either way, you're not fixing the issue.

Option 3 is the only way to go. Leadership requires accountability. Ultimately, the buck stops with you. It's hard, and practicing it builds trust. Team members know you have their backs. Colleagues know you'll take the necessary action to resolve problems, and when issues arise, you'll look at what role you played in it: Did you provide sufficient training? Were expectations clear? What additional resources did you fail to provide?

Look, it's not always easy. Sometimes you'll be very tempted to point fingers. It may be difficult to identify where you fell short, but adhering to this leadership principle will pay off. I promise.

... AND ALL I GOT WAS THIS LOUSY T-SHIRT

Your office's ambiance. The way your team engages patients. The questions you ask and how you listen—these are all part of the "upstream" sales process. The "downstream" process is just as vital to the success of your business. No one wants to be hung out to dry. No one wants to think, "I went to the dentist and all I got was this lousy appliance."

Curate an experience that leaves patients thrilled with their decision to proceed with treatment. Put yourself in their shoes. What would make you feel like you made the right choice?

Set clear expectations about follow-up appointments and inform patients what to expect each time. Use devices that have a nice presentation like ProSomnus or SomnoMed. Call the patient the day after delivery to check in. Consider a nice gift bag with cleaning tablets and a sleep mask. It doesn't have to cost much, but the feelings of goodwill and eventual referrals are priceless.

My homegirl, Angela is the marketer for a practice in The 100 Club. During the holidays, she drops off "Elf on the Shelf" dolls and baked goodies to referral sources. She encourages them to personalize their elves and make daily sleep-themed social media posts, along with hashtags for their respective practices. It's fun and inexpensive, it's personalized and attention-grabbing, and it generates buzz.

Personal touches like these create memorable experiences. Memorable experiences create rave reviews. Rave reviews generate referrals. Referrals turn into new patients. New patients convert to production. And so on. See how it works?

This is the ideal time to encourage your patient to write a Google review. Don't be overly pushy; just remind them how important these reviews are for providers and ask them to leave you a review today if it's convenient. Ideally, your team or an automated service will make it easy by texting patients a link for leaving reviews. Ask for referrals and make them feel good about their decision.

NOW WHATCHU GON' DO WITH IT?

You might think this could work for other dentists but not for you. "I'm double booked. I only have a couple minutes. Ain't nobody got time for that."

Nobody has time to create real human connections? Nobody has time to get to the root of another person's problems and help them live a better life? Nobody has time to listen to another person?

Forget altruism. Let's look at it purely from a business perspective. What is increased patient retention worth to you? How much are patient referrals worth? How much do you value positive online reviews? What's the value of engaged team members and lower employee turnover?

The cost of ignoring all this is astronomically high. The payoff for incorporating these concepts into your life is even higher, and the dividends will continue to pay throughout your lifetime. The confluence of communication, caring, and commerce will change your practice.

There's more than one way to skin a cat (why would anyone skin a cat?). Find out what works for you, what gets the best results and the most rewarding reaction. We aren't automatons. We're humans, with panache and personality. We are rock stars.

Hone your skills, at the practice, with patients, and with your team. Pump up these jams at home and the cocktail party - with your kids and your friends. Practice your chops with physicians and at study clubs. Present at civic group meetings about sleep health such as A.W.A.K.E. meetings. Consider joining Toastmasters International. Steel sharpens steel.

The first section of this book is intended to give you the motivation and mindset to take action. I want to eliminate false hope, establish realistic expectations, and prepare you for what's to come.

This second section has been centered on consultative communication, with a focus on the front wheel as a counterweight to your DSM technical proficiency. This should buttress what you learned in the first section.

The next section will build on the foundational principles you've read so far. This will put a name to a system the top practices use. You'll learn actionable operational principles that will ameliorate your dental sleep practice and help you build a sustainable business. Keep reading.

W.O.W. LESIA TIERNEY

Author's note: During her first fifteen years in sleep medicine, Lesia and her partner Dr. Stacey Layman cofounded both GoGo Billing and GoTo Sleep Center for CPAP Alternatives. Lesia serves as CEO and treatment coordinator for the latter's three Phoenix-area offices where they've treated thousands of OSA patients. She's lectured across the U.S., trained hundreds of practices, and made zillions of people smile with her raucous laughter and infectious energy. Lesia is also an atrociously off-key singer, an out-of-this-world amateur florist, my wife, and my muse. —Jason Tierney

I am the world's worst dental assistant, but I can sell air—literally. That's my job. Dental sleep and insurance knowledge are useful. Sales skills definitely help, but the most important trait of a sleep treatment coordinator is a genuine desire to help people understand how better sleep can improve their lives. It's also important to create a habit of excellence and a build a structured-yet-fluid flow so patients get the attention they deserve, and the dentist stays on schedule. The following is what my typical day as a sleep treatment coordinator goes a somethin' like this. . ..

The office books 30 or 60-minute consultations with me and schedules an hour for scanning so we can begin same-day treatment. Before greeting the patient, I review the diagnostic sleep test and the patient's responses to our questionnaire, with special attention to their chief complaint. I can make accurate assumptions quickly and set the tone based on that answer alone: "I don't want to die at night" or "Doctor Emdee recommended it" and, my favorite, "I don't want a divorce." There's also a list of common complaints, e.g., "Difficulty staying asleep" and "Feeling unrefreshed in the morning."

With a big smile, I introduce myself: "My name is Lesia, and I'm here to get to know you a little bit, review your sleep test and symptoms, connect some dots, explain how the treatment works, help you pick one out, and review your financials and insurance coverage. If this is something you want to do, we'll head over to the next room and get started with the doctor."

From there, everything depends on the patient. We might spend the full hour getting into a deep philosophical discussion; laugh so hard we are crying; cry so hard we are laughing; just cut to the chase and get to work; or shake hands and walk them out with a task to follow up later.

When reviewing the sleep test with a patient, I ask if anyone previously reviewed it with them. Even if the answer is "yes," typically no one has explained what happens physically when they are sleeping, what apnea does to their body, and how it disrupts their sleep quality—you know, the stuff that matters. Someone may have shown them the dots, but seldom does anyone explain how they're connected. That's my job.

I use my hands to depict the tongue's retrusion and obstruction of the airway, describing in simple terms how "the tongue drops back, and you may snore." Depending on their snoring questionnaire responses, I mention that it may not bother them, but their bed partner will wake up and hit them and make them roll over.

The problem is no laughing matter, but we use humor to make things more palatable e.g., "This is secondhand snoring and domestic abuse. It's bad enough your sleep is disrupted with your apnea but getting hit certainly does not help."

Then I describe the pathophysiology of an apneic event. Note that I'm using clinical terms with you, and I use lay terminology when talking with patients. This is no accident. I recommend you adopt this same approach.

"An obstructive apneic event is when the airway is completely shut off," I say, bringing my hands together to demonstrate a collapse. "Your airway closes completely for 10 seconds or more and the oxygen in your blood drops 3 percent or more. DING DING! This is an apneic event. A hypopnea is like plugging your nose and breathing through a coffee straw for ten seconds, resulting in a 3 percent drop in oxygen - DING! DING! Episodes when your brain doesn't signal to your lungs to breathe are called "central events." Looking at your test, you had 56 full closures, 105 "coffee straw" breathing events, and zero centrals, so congratulations, your brain is good."

Then we usually both laugh.

"Did anyone ever review your results and explain what happens to your body while you're having an apneic event?" In 98 percent of cases, the answer is "no." This is when the show starts. They're usually tired and fighting yawns, and so I amp up the funny.

"When you're sleeping, your consciousness is disconnected. An elephant could walk into your room and, if it walked quietly, you'd have no idea. While you're sleeping, your sub-conscious is the boss of your body. Unfortunately, the part of the brain that tells your heart to beat and your lungs to breathe can't say, "hey, get the tongue out of the airway!"

"Normally, you breathe in oxygen and breathe out carbon dioxide. When your airway is shut off, however, the carbon dioxide goes into your blood where the oxygen should be. Your brain notices the carbon dioxide buildup in your blood and thinks you're dying. Your fight-or-flight response kicks in, and your body releasing adrenaline and cortisol. The adrenaline goes to your heart, increasing your heart rate and asks the brain, "What's going on?"

Story time continues. "The brain says 'We're dying! Hurry, if there is any oxygen in this body, get it up to me pronto. If I don't get it, I'll die, and I'm taking you with me!"

The heart replies, "I'm on it" and your blood pressure goes up. Your body's fight-or-flight response can also cause you to clench and grind your teeth, which might help flex the airway open.

This is when I look closely at oxygen levels. I also look at the patient's health history and usually connect heartburn, GERD, and acid reflux to prolonged periods of apneic events and lower oxygen levels. "Your airway is like a dam. When the dam is open, the water flows freely, Shut the dam, and the water starts to back up. Your airway is similar. Your lungs are still trying to breathe, but when your airway is closed, pressure builds up and your stomach may get involved." Call me Thomas Edison because this is when the light bulb turns on for the patients.

Next, we dive deeper into the patient's symptoms which usually include issues such as waking up several times throughout the night, feeling unrefreshed upon waking, plus memory problems. Again, I'm connecting the dots—explaining how apneic events can cause or exacerbate these symptoms. I equate sleep cycles to a roller coaster: cycling up and down throughout the night from one stage to another.

"REM (rapid eye movement) sleep is when the hormones are being released, the ones that say, 'I'm happy,' such as serotonin. Others, including leptin and ghrelin are responsible for managing hunger, while testosterone says, 'Let's do it, baby!'"

"Your brain is also organizing information. In short, you get smarter while you sleep. Your brain reviews what you learned throughout the day, keeping what's important and discarding what isn't. REM sleep also plays a key role in your cells' repair processes, and your brain washes out amyloid plaques. Build-up of these plaques can lead to Alzheimer's, dementia, and Parkinson's."

I continue, "Imagine that every time you have an apneic event, whatever stage of sleep you're in, whatever work is being done stops, and you get pulled into a lighter stage of sleep while the body deals with the apneic event just in case you need to wake up."

I hold up models of the upper and lower teeth. "This isn't rocket science. It's basic physics. When you fall asleep, your lower jaw relaxes and falls backward. Your tongue is attached to the lower jaw, and so it goes with it, cutting off your airway. Meanwhile, your lungs are still trying to breathe. Unfortunately, your airway is being shut off as though you're being strangled. Our goal, then, is to move the jaw forward slightly. We just need to stabilize it and prevent it from falling back. This forward movement is similar to a modified chin thrust in CPR."

The number-one response I get from patients is, "Wow, that makes a lot of sense."

What next? I show them options for appliances. Mindful of regulatory and insurance issues, I describe how each device works and inform the patient of all the options, including discussions of comfort and efficacy, not just insurance coverage. I instruct the patient to select the appliance they want and slide that appliance toward me. I write the name of the device they selected on top of the financial agreement.

Finally, we review the benefits and financials. I pull up a form from my billing team and let the patient know what their insurance will cover and what their out-of-pocket cost is. I use the same financial agreement for all patients and handwrite their information, including deductibles and coinsurance into the relevant fields. Then I turn the page toward them and say, "If you'd like to get started today, go ahead and sign and date the form."

Sleep treatment coordinators need to be empathetic, entertaining, and charismatic. Their job is to help people by improving their quality of life. Ideally, this person has experience with consultative sales processes and critical thinking skills. They need to be able to recognize patterns and "read" people—body language, tone, and so on—so they can "mirror" them and jibe with their personalities. For employees who possess these traits and experiences, a bit of focused training can take them up a notch or three.

Hoping that an existing employee who doesn't have this mindset will somehow "get it" is a recipe for failure and a formula for firing.

We're all salespeople, and this is especially true for treatment coordinators, at least those of us who own our role every day. And when the sale involves a person's health and wellbeing, compassion and caring are essential. This is a crucial position in a dental sleep practice—any practice really—because time spent with an auxiliary employee is time saved for the dentist and other treatment providers.

SECTION 3

G.O. D.E.E.P

"A system is never the sum of its parts; it's the product of their interaction. The performance of a system doesn't depend on how the parts perform taken separately, it depends on how they perform together – how they interact, not on how they act, taken separately." —Russell Ackoff

You're proud of the roster of DSM lectures you've attended; courses presented by all the heavy hitters: Elliott, Carstensen, Spencer, Parker, Charkhandeh, Glassman, Tucker, Smith. You went to a couple mini-residencies and got accredited as a Diplomate *with two organizations.* You're traipsing along the yellow brick road to dental sleep success.

At least that's where you thought you were headed. You have an encyclopedic knowledge of the most popular devices and you've mostly figured out how to navigate the mind-numbing catch-22 commonly known as medical billing. No one knows more about starting positions But a few years later and you're only a couple steps down the road. What's the deal?

Listen to me. Put your phone down. Focus. Are you ready for the answer to your woes? It's time for another acronym.

You have to G.O. D.E.E.P.

First, let me spell it out and then define the critical importance of this process.

G. Generate a vision

O. Outline the path

D. Delegate appropriately

E. Execute

E. Evaluate

P. Pivot

Without exception, the most prolific DSM practices share the following traits:

- Charismatic communicators

- Dedicated sleep champion

- Clearly defined roles and responsibilities

- Empowered team members

- Aligned vision

- Commitment to the shared mission

- Engagement in the process

This gives dental sleep practices a replicable framework for success. Note that this process is applicable to nearly every business: from sleep practices and restorative offices to tattoo shops and scuba gear outlets. This is the scaffolding for you to build a bountiful, bumpin' business.

Now let's get ready like Kent Smith on a dive and G.O. D.E.E.P.

FIG. 13 "GENERATE A VISION"

GENERATE *VERB*

1. to bring into existence. 2. to be the cause of (a situation, action, or state of mind).

"Clarify your vision and you will make better decisions about people, processes, finances, strategies, and customers." —Gino Wickman

Many dentists want to treat more sleep patients. They see an opportunity to provide comprehensive care, help patients, add a profitable new procedure, and do something different. Oftentimes, the dentist is an apneic and their own first patient. Or it might be a friend or loved one. You know what happens next. It's happened to you. You're bitten by the sleep bug.

Based on my own experience and anecdotes shared by hundreds of dentists, the realization that you can make a huge difference in someone's life is a game-changer. It's like a drug; once you've felt that euphoria, you want more of it. With 25 percent of the U.S. adult population suffering from sleep apnea, you're excited about the possibilities of a sleep practice.

You have a purpose. A vision. A mission. You're a dentist renewed.

Meanwhile, the reception from your team is lukewarm. They halfheartedly nod their collective heads when you tell them about the great course on sleep apnea you just came back from. Maybe you even tell them you really want to make this an integral part of the practice. They can sense that you're serious. Their affirmative nods suggest that they "get it." They don't get it.

They chalk your passion up to a passing fad. It's happened many times before. If they can serve up unhealthy heaps of status quo, they reason, you'll forget about this sleep thing like you got hit with a *Men in Black* mind eraser. The misalignment of mission and vision is not unique to dentistry, either. Leaders must be able to see the vision, and the onus is on them to help others see it, too. Gino Wickman writes in *Traction*: "Leaders end up frustrated, staff ends up confused, and great visions are left unrealized." Don't let it happen to you, your patients, or your practice.

How can you change their attitudes? How do you generate buy-in and get the team to share your passion for an atelic mission?

There is a way, and it starts with your vision, your "why."

You've probably heard some variation of the "what's your 'why'" phrase over the past decade. Popularized by Simon Sinek's seminal book *Start With Why*, the phrase's underlying concept has reached cliché status, but you should still read it.

In his book, Sinek posits that people are inspired by a sense of purpose (their "why"), which should be communicated before the "how" (processes and methods) and the "what" (results or outcomes). Inspiration, not manipulation, is the more sustainable and impactful motivator.

Defining your "why" is vitally important to getting everyone onboard. It's imperative that you convey this to your team. At this stage, you're not talking about how easy sleep is going to be or how little disruption it will bring to your office. You're not talking about the workflow. That all comes with the "how."

Start by talking about the epiphany you had at the course. Share how your father passed away prematurely and how, if you'd known then what you just learned at the CE course, he'd still be alive. Open up about not wanting another daughter or son to suffer the way your family has. That's what you want to tap into. Your jaw should be clenched, your blood pressure rising, and your purpose laser-focused as you paint the picture of this vision for them.

Don't sandwich the talk between patients. Don't pass it along via the office manager. Don't mention it as an aside. Schedule a special team meeting to drive home that this is not business as usual. It's not a drill. This is for real.

Call it your purpose, your passion, or your "why." You're sharing your core with them. Infect them with your ardent altruism. Tell them. Show them. Paint a picture in vibrant color.

But you can't expect them to care about your dad as much as you do. They have to identify their own "whys." Fortunately, this is where you can provide guidance. Share personal stories that tug on their emotional heartstrings. Talk about celebrities who suffer from OSA, and highlight how the statistics translate to real life. For example, "We've got 16 patients coming in today. Statistically, four of them have sleep apnea and are at greater risk of heart attack and stroke. They're at increased risk of falling asleep behind the wheel and crashing into your kids' school bus. Devastated families will be left to pick up the pieces, but we can do something about it." They should believe this so deeply they want to get it tattooed on their foreheads.

Lead them through an exercise to identify their purpose. You might think this is just a step away from new age crystals or asking, "What's your sign?" If it sounds "woo-woo," it's not. It's a huge leap toward creating alignment, buy-in, and synchronicity. You're building a movement. Joey Reiman, CEO of BrightHouse, nailed this point with his statement that, "Revelation is the collision of information, intuition, and your highest values."

"WHY" EXERCISE?

During the team meeting, give everyone a pen and a sheet of paper with the first two questions printed on it. Leave enough space between the questions for them to write their answers. Give them a few minutes to answer each question.

1. What's important in life?

2. If I were to die today, how would I want to be remembered?

Ask each team member to share their answers. Oftentimes, their responses will focus on their kids or things like "being remembered as a good person, a good parent, and a good friend."

Ask them to consider the next question. Read it aloud to them and ask them to write down their responses.

3. What can I do at work today to support my answers to the first two questions?

Spend a few minutes sharing and discussing their responses. Be careful not to outwardly judge anyone's answers. Be kind. Be open. This is what's true to them at the moment and they're exposing their vulnerabilities.

Next, ask each of them to write their personal WHY statements beginning with "My WHY is _____," and empower them to share their creations.

If space allows, encourage everyone to place their personal WHY statements in a common area, where they're visible to everyone on the team. This will serve as a continual reminder and a springboard for camaraderie as you forge ahead in your shared mission. This newfound alignment will support your mission as you outline the path forward.

To get traction and drive meaningful long-term change to make it part of the practice's culture, its DNA, it is vitally important to over-communicate the WHY. Make sure everyone sees it regularly in the common area. Discuss it in team meetings. Add it to your website and incorporate it into your marketing materials.

Harvard professor John Kotter studied change agents and discovered that they tended to under-communicate the new intended direction. On average, the people tasked with leading organizational change communicated the change 10 percent as frequently as needed. Communicate and over-communicate. Then do it again. Ten more times.

If you think this stage is just feel-good nonsense, ignore it at your peril. Memorializing it on paper and making repeated impressions and recitations concretizes the concepts. Think back to your grade-school days: the flag in the classroom, the daily Pledge of Allegiance, U.S. history textbooks, the pop quizzes, and so on. All of these were aimed at inculcating you with the responsibility of citizenship and pride in being an American. You want your team to internalize the same commitment to your sleep practice mission.

Think this sounds wacky or cultish? You're right-ish. Cults are fanatically wrong about something while your practice is fanatically right about helping people.

Now that we've established WHY, it's time to go deeper, into the HOW.

The "how" is the mentality you need to take your sleep practice to the next level. Half-in/half-out is a waste of time, effort, and mental well-being. So many practices' sleep dreams die on the field of good intentions, after being led there by lackluster leaders. This won't happen to you. You've generated a vision and articulated it clearly to your team. They are now disciples of sleep. Now what?

Ask yourself, "Who am I? What do I want to be? Who do I want to become?" You're neither your past victories—top of the dental school class, high school runner of five minute miles, hopscotch queen in grade school—nor your past failings—last in your dental school class, past bankruptcy, or "I already tried this dental sleep thing and it just didn't work."

You are what you do right now. All your experiences have prepared you for this moment. If you're eating a super-sized-something-or-other, you're not a healthy eater. Downing a few shots at the bar? You're not living a sober life. If you're not screening patients and reaching out to physicians, if you're not contacting a sleep testing company, you're not on track for dental sleep success. Harsh? Maybe, but it's true.

The time to outline your path forward is now. I'll paraphrase Antoine de Saint-Expury here: A vision without an outline and execution is a pipe dream, sucker. Or as Stephen King once wrote, "The scariest moment is always just before you start. After that, things can only get better."

W.O.W. LEN LIPTAK

Author's note: Len Liptak's ingenuity, business acumen, and affability have secured his position on DSM's Mount Rushmore. Watching him craft the ProSomnus vision, harness resources, develop a stellar team, and execute each step of the way is like a masterclass in organizational excellence. Len labors to raise all DSM ships in the field by supporting new research, championing medico-dental collaboration, and developing innovative products. —Jason Tierney

What inspires a business to change the world? What moves a business to disrupt an industry by engineering higher performance products and services? What motivates a business to thrive in the face of adversities like COVID, geopolitical events, and economic crises? What drives a business to grow five times faster than a better funded competitor? What enables team members of a business to each make dozens of good decisions each day?

That "thing" is called a vision. A vision is a goal, a view of a better future, that motivates, focuses, aligns, and compels. A vision provides purpose and direction. A vision encapsulates the benefits realized from each incremental ounce of effort. A vision provides motivation to overcome adversity. And, for these reasons, a vision is usually the difference between success or failure, exceptionalism or mediocrity, and fulfillment or disappointment.

How might a business generate a vision? A vision can come from many places. There is no right or wrong answer. A vision is usually the output of a formal, or informal opportunity analysis. Opportunity analyses involve cross referencing unique market needs with the know-how and resources of the business' leader(s).

When we formed ProSomnus, our vision was to start up a company that could make a meaningful difference in the world. Sung Kim, Dave Kuhns,

Laing Rikkers, Mark Murphy, Heather Whalen, Jerry Vogel, Brandon Woltman, Greg Vogel, and I engaged in an opportunity analysis that identified the unmet needs of the obstructive sleep apnea market and cross referenced them against our team's portfolio of know-how, such as the invention, development, commercialization, and manufacturing of precision medical devices. Then we asked ourselves, if we apply our know-how to the obstructive sleep apnea market, can we achieve our vision of making a meaningful difference in the world? We then refined and tailored the specific wording of our vision accordingly.

Though it is essential to have a compelling, motivating, authentic vision, implementation is key. The famous Peter Drucker advises that culture eats strategy for breakfast. The oracle of Omaha, Warren Buffet, urges businesses to hire employees based on attitude over skills. The point is that the vision is more than just words. It is the DNA of the business. It is a way of life for the business. It is a guidepost for making decisions when data and logic paint an incomplete picture.

There are three components to implementing a vision. The first component is the "feet," or walking the walk. The second component is the "mind," or demonstrating that it is feasible to realize the vision. The third component is the "heart," or directly linking every action of every employee with the vision.

The "feet" component of implementing the vision requires the leader(s) to walk the walk, to lead by example, *to show* in addition *to tell*. The leader(s) must be willing to put in the same amount of time and passion that they expect from colleagues, if not more. The business leader(s) must consistently and authentically demonstrate that the vision is worthy of their time, their sacrifices, and their resources.

The "mind" component of the implementation involves making a rational argument that the vision can be realized. Colleagues want reassurances that their time, efforts and energies are translating into success. The main way we do this at ProSomnus is to celebrate progress. Progress can come in the form of a patient or provider testimonial. It can be the results of a clinical study or a patent allowance. It can be the achievement of important, internal milestones. Celebrate. Be inclusive. Be generous.

The "heart" component involves linking progress with specific contributions from each and every team member. At ProSomnus, every team member understands how their everyday activities support the production of our devices, which patients rely on for better sleep breathing. Members of team ProSomnus are not just operating a milling robot, or pushing a button in our design software, or in-servicing a referring physician for a dental sleep medicine provider. They are helping a patient live a longer, healthier life through our devices that enable better sleep breathing. They are not just operators or sales representatives or finance professionals. They are integral to helping patients live better lives.

Wrapping up; generate a vision that motivates you and your colleagues. Paint a picture of a better future. Check that the leader(s) have know-how that is relevant to achieving the vision. Memorialize it in writing, but make your vision transcend words by implementing it. Remember the "Feet" "Mind" and "Heart" when implementing a vision. Walk the walk to convince your colleagues that a vision is worth the effort. Demonstrate a vision is realizable by acknowledging and celebrating progress. Ensure that every team member understands how each of their daily activities contributes to realizing a vision. Good luck!

FIG 14 "OUTLINE THE PATH"

OUTLINE *VERB*

1. to draw the outline of. 2. to indicate the principal features or different parts of.

"You do not rise to the level of your goals. You fall to the level of your systems."
—James Clear

Your team doesn't know that you bought new medical billing software until the company calls to schedule onboarding training. Darkness descends. Who's using it? How are they using it? You did mention it, didn't you? Maybe not. They don't know how it's supposed to fit into their already busy days. What are they supposed to *stop* doing to free up the bandwidth to take this on?

What are the goals? What is the plan?

It's happened in the past, with a novel whitening method, clear aligner treatment, or whatever was being hawked at the meeting. Whether it was a product, service, or technology, no one else on the team heard the same message you heard. In this case, the shiny new object is dental sleep medicine. They can't see your vision, and you don't have time to share it with them because there's an emergency patient in operatory 2, Sam called in sick, and you're already 10 minutes late because you got stuck talking to your son's teacher about her toothache when you dropped him off at school.

Your team gets the feeling that, if they ignore it long enough, it'll fade away and something else will come along. Maybe you'll attend a different course and realize that the focus needs to be on boosting SRP production. Or 3D printing. And so on. Everything is different, but nothing has changed. They don't like living this way, and you hate it.

Sound familiar?

I encountered this *ad nauseam* when I ran a DSM software company. Doctors sign up for the course and like what they hear. They buy the software with high hopes for a profitable new procedure needed by so many patients. Then they charge into the office the following Monday only to get deluged with demands on their time. At best, the dentist makes a disjointed attempt to get their team onboard. At worst, they forget about it by the time the second patient is in the chair.

You're likely somewhere in the middle. You probably tried to squeeze in some conversations with your team about implementing DSM. You likely sat in on some of the software training sessions. Maybe you even insisted that you be involved in all those sessions. Then you got busy and had to reschedule. Interest waned, and so did your team's patience.

They didn't understand the vision and they definitely didn't see the outline of the path forward. It's like humming your favorite song in your brain, but it's only audible for 2 seconds out of every 20. You know the tune, but no one else does. You're asking the team to act like Clark Griswold and Cousin Eddie when they lost a nest egg playing 'Guess What Number I'm Thinking' in *Vegas Vacation*. You're smarter than that. We know our *why*. It's time to shift gears and focus on the *how*. We'll start by outlining the path and setting objectives. Let's make sweet music together.

OUTLINE = CHECKLIST = MAP

In *Checklist Manifesto,* Atul Gawande, MD writes about a community health clinic in Boston comprising more than 20 facilities with over 600 doctors covering 60 specialties. Using a "day-in-the-life" snapshot, Dr. Gawande shares that the labor ward asked him to see a 25-year-old with "mounting right lower abdominal pain, fever, and nausea, which raised concerns about appendicitis, but she was pregnant, so getting a CT scan to rule out the possibility posed a risk to the fetus." Then he's paged by a gynecological oncologist because a patient "with an ovarian mass that upon removal appeared to be a metastasis from pancreatic cancer." Next, an MD at another facility called to transfer a patient in ICU "with a large cancer that had grown to obstruct her kidneys and bowel and produce bleeding they were having trouble controlling." He continues with a litany of other varied demands on his time involving complex health issues. In summary, he notes that he had six patients with more than two dozen unique diagnoses.

Gawande goes on to make readers wince even more by enumerating the spread of complexity seen in a typical office setting. One physician. Twelve months. The patients seen in that interval have 250 primary diseases with 900 other active medical issues that must be considered. The MD prescribed approximately 300 meds, performed dozens of procedures, and ordered more than 100 tests. As a DSM practitioner, the maladies you're dealing with are different, but you're slammed. Like Dr. Gawande, you're interrupted continually with demands on your time, attention, and expertise.

The author is neither describing a nightmare, nor is he gloating, i.e., "you think you've got it bad ..." Rather, he's using his lens of medicine to acknowledge how complex many professions have become. EMRs, billing systems, administration, and human resources, and don't forget the patients.

More than 150,000 patients die each year post-surgery. The author devotes the remainder of the chapter underscoring the enormous impact a basic five-point pre-surgery checklist had on post-surgery infections:

1. Wash hands with soap.

2. Clean the patient's skin with chlorhexidine antiseptic.

3. Put sterile drapes over the patient.

4. Wear a sterile mask and gloves.

5. Put a sterile dressing over the insertion site once the line is in.

In more than 33 percent of surgeries monitored, at least one of these steps was skipped. After instituting the checklists—including requiring doctors to check off each one and encouraging nurses to intervene if a step was missed—infection rates plummeted from 11 percent to 0. After one year, the monitors estimated that 43 infections and 8 deaths were avoided, and millions of dollars were saved. All from emphasizing a simple, five-point checklist. Checklists emphasize necessary steps and provide memory prompts.

Maybe you're thinking, *that might work for them but not for me.* Or maybe you're thinking, *this is unnecessary.* Unsurprisingly, some of the book's study subjects felt the same way. Skeptics viewed the checklist studies as irrelevant because they only tracked one hospital, Johns Hopkins, which has access to abundant resources. Sinai-Grace, a downtrodden hospital in Detroit had more central-line infections than 75 percent of U.S. hospitals. Then it adopted the five-point checklist.

In the first three months, Sinai-Grace reduced its infection rate by two-thirds. Eventually, its infection rate dropped to zero. If they can save lives with lists, you can, too.

BULLET POINT
EXTRAVAGANZA

"If you fail to plan, you are planning to fail." —Benjamin Franklin

Everyone needs to know their position, the process, and the expectations. The "Who's-on-first, what's-on-second, I-don't-know-is-on-third" nonsense is the off-ramp to bail on DSM. Division of labor. Expectations. Accountability. These must be crystal clear.

Fortunately, there's a clearly defined path to a better tomorrow. There's no amorphous black hole. Everyone knows what they need to do, how they need to do it, and because you've all found your unique *why* together, everyone now knows why they need to do it. This is powerful.

We're going to outline the path to success. The vision was macro. We're going micro now. Deep into the weeds. Who's going to assist with sleep cases? How will you handle medical billing for treatment?

What about sleep testing? Who will you refer patients to for testing? How will you shore up the likelihood that those patients will come back to you when OAT is appropriate? Will you buy and dispense your own units? Who will interpret and diagnose? Will you use a service? How will you get new patients? Who will manage the financial discussion? What will it sound like?

Over the years, I've developed a couple devices, tons of CE events, a once-popular DSM symposium, and training continuums, among many other complex projects. Getting those devices from my brain into your patients' mouths required mechanical designs, regulatory protocols, marketing and sales, manufacturing processes, and many other un-sexy steps that nonetheless separate success from failure.

Maybe you attended the symposium I created. It was once hailed as the best meeting in DSM, heralded by attendees for the quality of speakers, breadth of vendors, and fun vibe. Finding a venue, using their AV or selecting an outside company, vendor outreach, catering costs, speaker scheduling, registration processes, costs, who will be where when, and on and on. Information was gathered, options weighed, and decisions were made.

We facilitated several team meetings to communicate updates, assign responsibilities, and solicit feedback. It's critical that your team is secure and comfortable speaking up and sharing their insights. This isn't a fiefdom. Ego is the enemy here. You might be the smartest person in the room, but all those other people can help you identify blind spots overlooked due to your hyper-focus. If you had a positive experience at the symposium, it wasn't an accident. It was a manifestation of the exercise you're about to go through. I used the same process to write each section and subsection of this book.

Creating the outline is a defined process. However, rigidity can be immobilizing. Flexibility and agility are keys to successful execution. Grab a notebook or open a Google or Word Doc. I'm going to make it super easy and proceed as I typically do, with a yellow legal pad and a cheap pen. You can create flow charts or Lucid charts, or use sticky notes like software developers, but you have to do it.

By pinpointing key objectives and identifying the moving parts, we can simplify complexities and define the path forward. Author Stephen Ambrose wrote of President Dwight Eisenhower, "Faced with a complex situation, he usually tried to separate it into its essentials, extract a principal point, and then make that point his guiding star for all decisions." Look, you aren't planning D-Day, you're trying to simplify practice protocols, and grow your sleep biz. You got this.

I encourage you to carve out the time to follow this process. There's strength in numbers. For this initial pass, though, I suggest you trek solo.

You're probably thinking, *But, Jason, two paragraphs ago you bloviated about the importance of a team effort.* True, but doing this initial exercise on your own will help clarify your thoughts. It will allow you to brainstorm freely— no concerns about offending a team member who might be omitted from the mission or decision-making. You'll lean into them later. For now, just write down everything that comes to mind. No step is too big or too small. Brain blitz!

List all the steps and processes that come to mind, free-form, freestyle. Just go. You're not looking for structure or chronology now. Just Jackson Pollock those ideas out there. If your practice is just getting into sleep, your nascent list might look something like this:

- How to get patients

- Which medical billing company and who sends them files?

- Sleep testing – buy or use company?

- Who's the sleep champion?

- Hire a new assistant or assign to Tiffany?

- How will the front desk answer the phone?

- Look into referrals from ENTs across the street?

- Can Janet learn enough about sleep to market to MDs?

- What do I charge?

- Do I need software?

- How do we become Medicare providers?

- What changes do we need to make to our practice insurance policy?

This is by no means an exhaustive list, but it has some of the common items that have come up when I've conducted the exercise with other dentists.

Next, write each item at the top of its own sheet of paper, or give it a first-level bullet point if you're using a Word Doc. Then create sub-bullets for each item and sub-sub-bullets. These second and third-level bullets should get increasingly granular. Dive deep, like Mariana Trench deep from the main bullet. Don't think about it too much. Just keep writing.

Your list might look something like this:

- How to get patients
    - Get team trained on signs and symptoms
        - Online training?
        - Go to a course?
        - Contact company for in-service?
    - Screen all hygiene patients
        - Ask Dr. Erin Elliott which forms she uses
        - Ensure new *AND* existing patients complete the form
    - Get patient brochures
        - Have April order from the appliance labs?
        - Make our own?
    - What is protocol if we see signs/symptoms?
        - How will we prevent schedule falling behind?
        - Who talks about it with patients?
            - Me?

- RDH?
- Sleep champ?
  - What is the script?
    - SAY:
      - Research shows …
      - Have you had a home sleep test?
      - What treatment have you previously tried?
    - DON'T SAY:
      - We can cure sleep apnea
      - CPAP is bad
      - Don't quote fees over the phone
- Get medical referrals
  - Ask for lunch with ENT across the street
  - Find out what April's husband Kenny does when their patients won't wear PAP – opportunity there?
- Marketing
  - Add posts to our social media
  - How do we get sleep added to our website?
  - Should we change our ValPak to a sleep consult?

After you've created several pages of lists, put them away. Sleep on it, and plan to revisit the lists tomorrow. Then you can clean them up, so they look like finished to-do checklists.

The examples listed above might seem elementary to more experienced DSM clinicians. If this is you, keep in mind that you can still benefit from this process even if you know the ropes. Your list's focus might be narrower—say, one or two primary categories—but the secondary bullet points will help you identify options, uncover opportunities, and recognize areas of weakness.

It'll serve as a "pre-mortem." Ask yourself, if this initiative fails, what will be the most likely reason for the failure? After identifying those compromised areas, we can fortify against them.

Let's say your aim is to find new marketing solutions for your DSM practice. Your list might look something like the one below:

- Contact Dr. Kent Smith and Dr. Stacey Layman to find out what they're doing
    - Online vs. offline marketing?
    - Costs?
    - Recommended companies?
- Reach out to the two marketing companies I met at last year's AADSM meeting
    - Cost and timeline?
    - How are they different from each other?
    - Any guarantees?
    - Who on our team will need to support this?
    - How much of my time will it take?

- o How are results tracked?

- o Who/how do they target?

  - ▪ PAP noncompliant?

  - ▪ Medicare demographic?

  - ▪ Income and other demographics?

- Should I do online vs. offline marketing or a hybrid?

  - o Coupon packs like ValPak?

  - o Geo-targeting?

- How do they access our social media accounts?

  - o Who has the passwords and admin for these?

  - o Which other profiles do we need to create?

Your outlines probably won't look like turn-by-turn GPS instructions. If that's what you're looking for here, you still don't get it. Your practice is unique, but these suggestions are like a well-worn path. You can stray from it a bit if you see something interesting, but keep the path in sight. E. L. Doctorow said the following about writing, but it's relevant here, too: "… [it's] like driving a car at night in the fog. You can only see as far as the headlights, but you can make the whole trip that way."

You will get there.

IFTTT

Now it's time to get your team together to review your outline. Until now, you've been working solo. Don't worry, be happy. It's not going to be an endless time sink. The bulk of your time will be dedicated to coordinating the front-end processes. Start by sharing your outline with your team and soliciting candid, constructive insights. Encourage your people to poke holes in it and think about what won't work, why, and how the issue can be resolved. You're sure to shake out at least a couple of good suggestions and tenable solutions. Your team's perspective will help identify snags that weren't on your radar. They can offer to take on certain tasks to move things forward.

A couple of weeks pass, and you ask how things are going with the sleep program. You don't get the responses you were hoping for. What seemed like a reasonable roadmap at the end of your kickoff meeting might not have been enough. Silence while nervous eyes dart around the room. The office manager pierces the white noise, "Um, we're working on it. Anitra is on maternity leave, so we've been running behind with everything."

Disappointed but hopeful, you inquire further, "Do we have info to look at for the marketing plans?"

"Nothing yet, but we will soon", she replies.

How did this happen? You *knew* you were on the cusp of a big breakthrough. What's the holdup? The team might be unclear as to who's responsible for which activities and when they need to be completed. Their goal, to gather information for external marketing initiatives, might *seem* straightforward, but essential details are missing, raising more questions than you've answered.

For example, whose job is it to call Doctors Layman and Smith? How should information from the call be documented? By when should it be completed? Are they expecting the call?

Not to worry; it's all part of the process. Follow these four steps when discussing assignments in future meetings:

1. Be specific and concrete. Explicitly state the goal, e.g., "April, call Dr. Layman by Friday to learn about the marketing companies she uses."

2. Break the goal down into individual tasks.

3. Elaborate on these tasks with details such as deadlines, who owns the task, how it'll be documented, and any other relevant details. It's like caulking cracks so nothing leaks through them.

4. Recap the action items, deadlines, etc., and get everyone's assent.

This process will go a long way in clarifying expectations. Making this a mainstay of how you'll proceed will result in it becoming second nature for everyone. You'll save tremendous amounts of time and money, which many organizations squander on ill-defined initiatives. Time to take it to the next level.

S.M.A.R.T. @$$

This clever acronym was introduced by George Doran, Arthur Miller, and James Cunningham in their 1981 *Management Review* article, S.M.A.R.T. goals present a simple, reproducible way to create benchmarks and delineate roles.

It stands for Specific, Measurable, Attainable, Relevant, and Timely.

S.M.A.R.T. goals minimize ambiguity and let people know exactly what's expected of them. This helps with the annual review process, salary increases, termination, and daily processes. You owe it to your team to let them know what the benchmarks are. This ensures accountability, objectivity, and clarity.

What does this look like in your practice?

S.M.A.R.T. goals with your front-desk team, Isabella and Regan, might sound like this:

- Currently, we're screening patients sporadically for sleep disordered breathing. Beginning Monday, you should start providing the Epworth Sleepiness Scale to every adult patient, new and existing.

- Right now, we're averaging 16 patients per day. That means we should have at least 250 patients screened by the end of the month.

- This will ensure that our patients get screened for this potentially harmful disorder, we can get the appropriate ones on the path to treatment, and we'll begin to implement DSM in a real way in our practice. Isabella and Regan, are you up for the challenge?"

Reviewing S.M.A.R.T. goals with your sleep coordinator, Tanya, might go something like this:

- "Tanya, right now we're getting an average of three patient referrals per month from Dr. Khalil, three from Dr. Blixt, and sporadic referrals from Dr. Kalantzis at Lakeview Sleep. We averaged eight total referrals per month last year.

- We need to bump up this number to 20 referrals per month by the end of this year. Please visit those three offices I just mentioned once a month with lunch or just a drop-in to keep us top-of-mind. I also expect you to visit at least two new potential referral sources each week.

- During our first sleep huddle each month, you'll provide us with an update on referral figures, your visits from the previous month, and any relevant details for those coming up."

Do you see what we did in each of those examples?

We gave specific numbers, goals, and instructions. There was no ambiguity in those examples.

There are measurable goals with clear, quantifiable metrics.

Although each of these examples includes significant goals, they are definitely attainable. The goals shouldn't be too easy; they should stretch each team member's abilities. However, they do need to be attainable. Otherwise, they become demoralizing. In the referral example, if the sleep coordinator is tasked with generating 100 new referral sources each week, she will fail every week until eventually she becomes a source of dissension in the practice or strolls out one final time - middle fingers waving the entire way.

These examples also provide relevant goals. It's not about doling out busy work just to give people something to do. The goals mentioned—increasing the number of screened patients and boosting the volume of referring physicians—are both relevant, even paramount, to the success of your dental sleep practice.

On an episode of Azeem Azhar's *Exponential View* podcast, Tony Fadell, co-creator of the iPhone and iPod, talked about how individual departments at Apple had to get aligned with the company's mission. Each department was operating as its own business unit with its own metrics and goals, and so many units hit their individual bonus goals even though the company was in the red. Individuals and departments should have their respective S.M.A.R.T. goals, but they must move the practice toward your overall goals.

Finally, the goals are timely. They're associated with deadlines. It's been said that "a goal without a deadline is a dream." Imposing a deadline goes a long way toward achieving the goals, and it's necessary for accountability. If you want to know why you're not hitting your goals, take a look at your deadlines.

As a last note on this topic, remember when you told Tanya that you expected her to share a status update during the first huddle of the month? That wasn't an aside; it's important. Renowned business management consultant Peter Drucker famously declared, "What gets measured gets managed."

We're going to take it a step further with what's known as Pearson's Law, which states, "That which is measured improves. That which is measured and reported improves exponentially." This is a truism, and it adorns the walls of executive coaching offices and coffee mugs on boardroom tables around the globe.

Now we've generated a vision and gotten aligned as to why we're doing this. We've outlined a path forward, and we have the tools we need to establish clear performance.

Are you going to do it all yourself? Of course not. You've gotta let go. It's time to delegate, but first, let's check out some words of wisdom from one of my favorite human beings, Dr. Max Kerr.

W.O.W. MAX KERR

Author's note: Dr. Max Kerr is undoubtedly one of the best to do it. His multi-site practice, Sleep Better Austin provides comprehensive sleep services to patients throughout the greater Austin area. His disciplined focus self-improvement and self-actualization is truly inspiring. Additionally, he's an excellent clinician with a love for his family that is second to none. Dr. Kerr is funny, engaging, kind, and he's a certified EOS Implementer. I can honestly say that I love this man. —Jason Tierney

We rely upon three pillars to ensure that we grow effectively without losing quality of patient care: trust, structure, and follow-up.

Trust: Trust within a business is similar to a nice roux. It has minimal ingredients, it's difficult to perfect, and it's extremely easy to screw up. The first ingredient of trust in a business is trust of oneself. The leader-doctor must trust that they know the direction to take the business along with what's best for the business. This requires an intense desire for personal growth and deep questioning of oneself. If you don't trust yourself, then no one will.

Second, you have to trust the team you've built. There's no substitute for time. Knowing team members for some time creates predictability. Promoting from within whenever possible is good. When building team trust, vulnerability is key. When team members see that the leadership is willing to own mistakes, they lose the fear of being reprimanded. I am always the first to take the blame, which empowers the team to speak up, bring ideas to the table, and share critical feedback.

Third, when something does go wrong, when a team member messes up or an initiative crashes, make sure that you recover productively. This is where controlling emotions comes in handy; nothing shuts down a great team faster than an angry outburst from the leader when something doesn't go as planned. When you trust yourself, when you've developed trust in your team, when you have confidence that when you mess up you'll learn and get better, delegation becomes an opportunity instead of an obligation.

Structure: Structure starts with the end goal in mind. Define your business's focus, your long-term goals, and your intermediate goals, and then devote time to each.

We have 90-minute weekly meetings and full-day quarterly meetings to ensure that we're still focused on the right goals. We take bite-sized chunks (or initiatives) of the overall goal and commit to the team to complete them. It's also important to "bake in" regular times to give and receive feedback with individual members of the team.

We have quarterly one-on-ones with team members, and they take on an informal tone. We discuss wins over the past quarter, areas for improvement, and ways to be better leaders to further support the team. A business that has constructed a solid foundation of direction, regular team communication, and sanctified feedback provides fertile structure for scalability and delegation.

Follow-up: Once you've developed trust within your sleep business and a structure that guides everyone, your next step is the scariest: delegation. Each quarter, our leadership team evaluates what tasks are not our highest priority and ask our direct reports to help with or totally take over these tasks. This simple exercise keeps the most valuable doing the most valuable while empowering our direct reports.

But delegation without "inspecting what we expect" is like spitting in the wind. We have to be clear about expectations and deadlines, and then we have to follow-up at delivery time with productive feedback.

Because it's easy to forget this step, I put reminders in my phone for when and what to follow-up with. We also use a project management software that tracks to-dos.

Once you and your team have focused on building trust among yourselves and each other, create a supportive organizational structure, and delegate the right way, your business will begin to grow and take on a life of its own. This growth also requires an evolution of leadership. As practice owners, our value is often defined by how productive we can be ourselves. When scaling our business, our value becomes defined by how productive we can make our direct reports and their teams.

FIG. 15 "DELEGATE"

DELEGATE *VERB*

1: to entrust to another

2: to assign responsibility or authority

"Every kingdom divided against itself is brought to desolation; and every city or house divided against itself shall not stand." —Matthew 13:25

BULLS HIT

In the midst of an historic three-peat run, the 1993 Chicago Bulls' legendary coach, Phil Jackson took the court to play against the Phoenix Suns. Everyone watched in astonishment as Coach Phil took the court in his suit and tie. It was weird, like, *really freaking weird*. He in-bounded the ball to himself. The ref blew the whistle. Possession changed. Phil guarded Charles Barkley and then jogged over to the sidelines and screamed at himself to guard Danny Ainge. Dumbfounded, the Suns in-bounded the ball and dunked away.

Finally, mercifully, the buzzer sounded. Game over.

It should have been a forfeit. Everyone knew he didn't stand a chance, but what could anyone do? Phil Jackson was the head coach. Sure, one or two players nervously stammered up to him pre-game that this was not advisable. A couple others even planned a mutiny. They lambasted his decision behind his back. They courted other teams and fanned trade rumors. Michael Jordan got so flustered he gave up the sport entirely and started playing baseball. The Bulls lost, Phil Jackson never regained the respect of his players, season ticket holders canceled their subscriptions, and every Bulls fan began rooting for the Lakers.

If this isn't the way you remember it, that's because it never happened. Sounds stupid though, huh? Why would the head coach try to play the game while also coaching, especially when he had an all-star team? All they needed was coaching.

How is this different from the choices dentists across the United States make every damn day?

Maybe you don't have an all-star team just yet. So, create one. As illustrated in the Coach Phil example, doing all of it yourself is untenable, unsound, and frankly speaking - a very bad idea.

Let's propound on this idea. A patient's entire OAT journey in your office takes no more than 60 minutes end-to-end. That's probably not the way it works in your practice right now, but it's the goal—a readily attainable, totally realistic goal.

You might be wondering how this is only going to take an hour. Maybe you've heard some guru pontificate about the benefits of their three-hour new-patient exam. I hope that's not you. If it is, go read *The Brothers Karamazov* to learn the alphabet.

You're focused on optimizing care so you can get the best patient outcomes and maximize profit. That's where your team comes in. They'll manage most of the patient journey in your practice, and that means you'll have to invest in them. I know, you've spent money on assistants to go to expanded-function training or took them all to a CE course on a cruise ship and then one of them quit the following week. Stuff happens, but the likelihood of bumps along the way is not a reason to forego the journey altogether.

You have to delegate. You gotta have the right team members and equip them with the education, tools, and resources they need to propel this piece of your business. Then you need to empower them with the autonomy to manage these processes. Don't micromanage them. Micromanaging:

1. Stresses you out

2. Destroys trust and morale with the team

3. Kills your DSM dreams

Just one more 90s-era basketball reference: "You have to create your Dream Team."

Everyone on the team has a role, but there's overlap. Switching sports, sometimes the running back throws up a block. Sometimes they catch a pass and pick up some receiving yards. If the QB fumbles the snap, the running back better give chase to stop that DB lumbering down the field with the ball.

It's all his job. There is nothing that isn't that RB's job. And when you give him the ball and a hole in the line, it's cool to just sit back and watch the magic happen.

Dental sleep medicine is a team sport. Your team should be composed of all-stars, but it has to be a team. Phil Jackson was a Hall of Fame coach. So are you. Michael Jordan is a legend. Your sleep champ will be, too. Pippen was a laudable assistant. And so is your assistant. The convergence of these icons resulted in a team for the ages. The same can be true of your DSM dream team.

DON'T SLEEP ALONE

"No person will make a great business who wants to do it all himself..."
—Andrew Carnegie

There's no definitive recipe about how to treat every patient, which appliance to use for each one, or which paperwork will be needed for every insurance claim. You must learn the foundational information, think critically, and include the appropriate subject matter experts on your team, both your internal and external teams. This might entail delegating impressions to your highly capable assistant and entrusting your medical biller to fight the claim denial. You can't do it all. It's imperative that you build a team of all-stars.

You want to be involved. You want to support your team, boost your knowledge base, and understand what's going on at each step. That's admirable, but, taken to the extreme, it's the reason you're unlikely to ever achieve real DSM success.

You start out as the most astute student. You ask the software trainer good questions and constantly seek opportunities to streamline the sleep testing process. You admit it when you don't grasp the Byzantine workflow that the medical billing company is proposing. You're a primary driver of the sleep program's success to date. It's your biz for frickssake.

But now you've grown from one patient per month to four or five. That's a good thing, right? Yes, but it also means more challenges. There are additional moving parts, more opportunities for things to fall between the cracks. As Biggie Smalls famously rapped, "Mo' money. Mo' problems."

Until now, your superpower has been your astonishing ability to learn so much in so little time and do a bunch of extra sleep stuff without screwing with the schedule too much. Still, that superpower needs to evolve into something greater if your sleep practice is going to grow and you're going to retain your sanity. The days of you doing everything are over. This doesn't mean that you're now hands off or your work is done, but that your work is *different*.

You'll lead, cultivate, and develop. Mostly, you'll serve as the nerve center, - the ombudsman, the single source of truth - but not as the doer of all things. You've graduated to a role in which you're working *on* the business instead of *in* the business.

We complain about the many demands on our scarcest resource: our time. But then, inadvertently, we insert ourselves into nearly everything. Or we insist on being the keeper of tribal knowledge. We become the bottleneck, prohibiting others from acting until we've given our blessing—which we're always too busy to give since we're always too busy. It's a vicious cycle, and we need to stop it.

The onus is on leaders to delegate meaningfully and appropriately, but what does this mean? Won't everything fall through the cracks? Won't the prisoners take over the jail? Won't you lose all control?

What constitutes effective delegation? What can you hand off and what should you retain? It's possible to eliminate the concerns and keep the train on the tracks. With an empowered team and effective delegation, we can go further faster, with less energy expended.

Simply stated, we must empower our teams by granting them the autonomy and latitude to make decisions. We have to equip them with the resources they need to do their jobs and move toward the agreed upon goals. And then we need to step aside so they can do their jobs. And you can do yours.

Your team will develop their skills as they realize greater career and personal development. Your business will be propelled forward as you'll be running on more engines with less thrust required from each. You'll have more efficiency and more sanity. You'll have more bandwidth to focus on important issues instead of focusing on pedantry.

As former Microsoft exec Steven Sinofsky opined, "When you delegate work to a member of the team, your job is to clearly frame success and describe the objectives." If this line of thinking sounds familiar, it's because it alludes to the steps we've described up to this point.

ROW, ROW, ROW YOUR BOAT

"If everyone is moving forward together, then success takes care of itself."
—Henry Ford

Your dental sleep practice is a rowboat, not one of those lame pedal boats tourists take out on the pond. Those things are like the dentist that does their own hygiene, takes out their own trash, and is defeated by the weight of bills before collapsing at the end of the day to watch *Dancing with the Stars*.

Nah, man. That's not you. Your DSM practice is like the shells the rowing teams use to glide above the water. Flying. All smooth motion in unison. Sinew, muscle, and endorphins. Seemingly effortless. This is what it's like when you have the right team. Before we can talk about the right fit for these positions, let's talk about the positions themselves.

You're the captain, but if you row that bad mutha solo, you'll end up shouting expletives at yourself while moving in a slow circle. You can't do it alone, cap'n.

Who do you need aboard? Who will impel you toward the goal and not just weigh you down?

You need someone in front, someone in back, and someone to glue it all together. Depending on your goals, your patient volume, and the strength of your sleep team, along with some additional variables, all of these "someones" might add up to anywhere from one to three people. Let's take a closer look.

A solid front-office person is a must-have. Their duties include answering the phones; scheduling referrals and new-patient appointments; managing existing patient interactions; gathering insurance information; managing insurance pre-authorizations; ensuring that you have the necessary documentation, such as sleep test reports; and of course, billing and collections. There's a lot of work to be done, but you can't tolerate any dead weight because it'll just slow you down.

A world-class assistant is worth their weight in serendibite. Their days will be spent taking impressions, scans, and bite records; assisting in device deliveries and adjustments; checking in cases from the lab and sending out new ones; uploading titration HST results; and back-office communications.

Can one person cover all the responsibilities listed here—one person doing the work of two people? If you have an exceptionally dynamic team member and you're only working one or two days per week, this could be feasible. If you're working more than two days a week, however, you'll need two team members for these two roles. If you're thinking you can't afford to do it now or your person is the exception, you're wrong. These aren't payroll expenditures. They're investments in your future.

Now you have kick-@$$ front office and back office covered. What about a sleep champion, sleep ambassador, sleep coordinator, or sleep whatchamacallit?

Here's one word describing sleep champions: *necessary.*

Here are a few hundred additional words. Lecturers including Dr. Mark Murphy and Dr. Jason Doucette teach that this is an irreplaceable role. The sleep champion's taxonomies vary by office. In some offices they function as the de facto office manager, while in others they supplement the front/back-office players and own the treatment coordinator's duties, too.

One dentist's treatment coordinator with a bevy of additional responsibilities is another dentist's sleep champion. Naval Ravikant could've been talking about the making of a sleep champ when he said, "The best jobs are neither decreed nor degreed. They are creative expressions of continuous learners in free markets." I'm not here to lobby for naming rights to the role. The fact is, titles are mostly unimportant. What's vitally important is that this individual oversees screening, testing, and relationship management. The sleep buck stops with them. They have their fingers on the pulse of each moving part in your sleep practice. They might prefer the front to the back-office (or vice versa), and that's fine, but they have to know what's going on and be willing and able to jump in anywhere. They're equally adept at talking shop with your billing company, discussing referral volume with Dr. Stu Pidaz's staff, and explaining how OAT works in a new patient consultation.

Patients don't fall through the cracks because the sleep champion doesn't let it happen. Lab cases don't go missing because they're on top of things. You don't have to cancel a day of deliveries because your assistant called in sick. Sleep champion to the rescue.

With you at the helm, your top-notch assistant and front desk superstar rowing in perfect unison, and your gold medal sleep champ doing their thang, you'll reach mobilized equilibrium. You'll move in tandem and get where you're going faster.

WHAT'S THAT SMELL?

"Nothing will kill a great employee faster than watching you tolerate a bad one."
—Perry Belcher

At one point, it might have been delightful. Not now. Now it stinks. Your first patient of the day mentioned it, and most of your team is holding their noses, *eeewwwing* and *guuhhhrossing* all morning.

Someone hid their grilled blue cheese sandwich in the recesses of the break room fridge too long, and now the office reeks. You wouldn't keep it in there just because it'd been there for a long time. Ignoring it isn't an option.

"I've tried stuff like this before, and my team wouldn't get on board," Dr. Alotta Excuses dismissively derides. Read between the lines of Dr. Excuses' derision and we find out what she really means. Her team has run roughshod for far too long. It's likely they do what they want, how they want, when they want, with intentions that are incongruent with the practice's purpose. They keep their resumes current because they hate their jobs and Dr. Excuses is, well, unpredictable.

Dr. Excuses' sinking ship has about as much chance at growing sleep as those grifter appliances have at growing bone, but a blue ocean of opportunity lies before you. Your team has abundant untapped potential.

The crystal ball tells me there's probably someone on your team who was good at some point, maybe even great. But like that sandwich, they're past their time in your office, and most of your team is put off by their behavior. Some patients have even complained. They've been coached, and you hope they'll change, but you're merely prolonging the inevitable. In *Thing Again*, Adam Grant writes, "You can lead a horse to water, but you can't make it think." You're also risking that this cancer on your business will metastasize.

These people need to become part of your past. It's not mean; it's the opposite. Allowing non-performers to overstay is a lose-lose proposition every time. There are no exceptions. Letting them go liberates them to seek an employer who's better suited for them. The disenchanted person gets their wish to be out of your office, and you can find someone who's a better fit. This is a win-win-win, and your only regret will be that you didn't cut the cord sooner. They'll be better off at Status Quo Dental over on Average Avenue. They can do their thing without the pressure of high expectations, and you can move faster after dropping the millstone. Later, we'll talk about finding and developing the right people, but first we have to eliminate the wrong ones.

You're encouraged to consult with an attorney or human resources professional when making employment decisions. I'm not an employment attorney, but I have terminated team members in a few states. The causes ranged from poor performance and drunkenness to theft and racist verbal attacks.

When terminating team members, I always follow the same process. First, I create a document detailing specific occurrences, including dates, that led to the termination. I include any performance improvement plans that were shared and the failed corrective actions. The documents avoid personal judgments or character assessments. Everything is centered on behaviors and actions. I also compile any relevant COBRA paperwork and severance information.

Terminations should take place at the beginning of the person's shift. It's a good idea to have the office manager, sleep champion, or other trusted person present. They'll serve as a witness but should not chime in during the proceeding. Bring the witness and two copies of the termination document into a quiet room away from patients and the rest of the team. Then bring the team member into the room. Be firm and direct, but professional and kind.

Tell them you need to have a crucial conversation. Hand them a copy of the termination document, and read it to them calmly. Inform them that today is their last day. If they argue or refute the claims, simply inform them the decision has been made, and it's not open for debate. Do not further justify your decision, and do not engage in additional dialogue, regardless of their response. Then ask them to sign the termination agreement. Finally, have the witness take them to gather their belongings and escort them off the premises. Thank them for their service and say good-bye. Depending on your unique practice situation, all of this can be performed by the office manager without your presence.

At the end of the day, gather the team together. Share with them that the individual is no longer with the practice. Don't share specific details. They probably already know. Let them know that you appreciate each of them and explain which tasks they'll need to absorb in the near-term and provide relevant updates regarding new hire plans. Finally, assure them that their jobs are secure and that a bright future lies ahead, and remind them how thankful you are for their commitment to excellence.

You read about the five whys concept in the previous section, and its application to this problem can be very telling. Start with why the terminated team member had to be let go. Then keep asking, "why?" You might realize that they didn't receive sufficient training. You may see that you ignored red flags during the interview process, or that the position was poorly defined. Maybe they were hired for not being obviously weak rather than strengths, or perhaps they were managed by an incompetent supervisor. Once you identified the root cause, you can fix the problem and minimize the likelihood of a recurrence. None of these steps are easy, but they are necessary. Jerzy Gregorek summed it up nicely on *The Knowledge Project* podcast with Shane Parrish, "... easy decisions, hard life. Hard decisions, easy life." You do what you need to do.

PMA

"If we get the right people on the bus, the right people in the right seats, and the wrong people off the bus, then we'll figure out how to take it someplace great." —Jim Collins

If I had a dollar for every time dentists have told me their teams "don't want to do sleep" or complain about how "insurance won't pay so no patients move forward", I'd have enough to buy a 2013 Camry with 135,277 miles on it.

The problem isn't which bite technique you're using, the labyrinthine medical insurance maze, or the STOP-BANG. To be sure, there are issues with each of these, but the major issue we can address for the good of your patients, your profitability, and your practice is... (cue Europe's *The Final Countdown* keyboard riff)

YOUR TEAM!

Do you have the right team members in the right roles? Outfitting your team with the right people is crucial to your success. You can't do this alone, and you can't do it when you're plagued by inefficiency and incorrigible or incompetent team members. They'll leave you drained, discontented, and stymied. There's a hilarious video online depicting three professional soccer players taking the field against a hundred schoolchildren. Swarms of kids chase after the ball while the pros artfully move it downfield. Pass, dribble, pass, header. One of the pros shoots. GOOOOAAALLL! Selecting the right three employees doesn't mean they can do the work of one hundred team members, but I think you get the picture.

A great vision without great people to execute the plan is like a tree without branches. To build the dental sleep practice of your dreams, you need to first ensure that the right people are in the right seats, on the right bus.

Because DSM is an emergent niche field, it's unlikely that you'll be able to hire an experienced sleep assistant. It's even less likely that you'll be able to identify a sleep champion with a proven track record. What will you do? Quit before you start?

Of course not.

James Baron and a team of sociologists found that hiring a professional with specific transferable skills triples the likelihood that a business will fail. Poaching a star employee from another practice is also tied to a high failure rate. However, hiring someone with character, commitment, and cultural fit is likely to lead to success. The right person with the right energy and a history of continual learning can be the missing link. Positive mental attitude (PMA) goes a long way.

Where do you find these people? Anywhere. I've hired DSM team members just about everywhere. The clerk whose checkout lane you prefer at the grocery store because they quickly get you through the line even when you have an overflowing cart and a 50 lb. bag of dog food. If you're like me and you just have a container of strawberries and a jar of peanut butter, you'll still wait behind the person with the cart that's like a leaning tower of groceries just so you can yap with the personable clerk for a minute. Their energy is infectious.

Can you picture that person checking in a new patient or scheduling an appliance delivery? Use your imagination.

Or the barista at your favorite coffee shop. You've seen them effortlessly juggling nine complicated drink orders with an average of twelve ingredients each. And they still remember your name. You feel seen. Acknowledged. Important. Can you envision this individual making your patients feel the same way during a consultation?

Imagine her discussing a patient's sleep study results with the same gusto and ebullience that she so flawlessly demonstrated when serving up your half-caf-mocha-wocha-skinny latte.

Of course, both the clerk and the barista will need training. They'll need to learn what AHI is, how to interpret sleep test results, and lots more. It's not a trivial undertaking. But for someone who has the wherewithal to learn all those drink orders or the ever-changing produce SKUs and what aisle they keep moving the beef jerky section to, they can certainly master the ins and outs of your burgeoning sleep practice. They have strong front wheels. You can help pump up their back wheels. Together, you can go far. Fast.

ROLE DESIGNS

WHAT ARE THEY GOOD FOR?
ABSOLUTELY EVERYTHING!

Interview three people about past gigs and at least one will babble about how the job's daily duties were dramatically different from what they were hired to do. Role designs disabuse employees from this notion. I'm using the term "role designs." You may have also heard them referred to as "job descriptions" or "job designs." Tomato. Tomahto. Whatever.

A "role design" is a simple document, usually just one page, describing the basic purpose of the role—its why—and then bulleting out each of the functions and responsibilities. Putting these documents together isn't busy work, and it shouldn't be done haphazardly. It's a crucial exercise, and the final documents will help guide your hiring process, performance reviews, and much more.

A sample role design for a dental sleep assistant appears on the next page. It it's not written in stone; it's guidance. Take what you want and leave the rest, but you ignore this crucial step at your peril (BTW, my computer just auto-suggested 'perio' instead of 'peril').

If you want to ensure the candidate you're considering for sleep assistant can do the J-O-B, all you have to do is compare their capabilities with those on the role design. If you decide that the sleep champion seems more like a sleep amateur and it's time to part ways, you can simply point to the role design to identify the performance deficiencies. What's required of the role that's not being done? Can you see how these steps can help with roles and delegation?

Dental Sleep Assistant Role Design

Title: Dental Sleep Assistant

Summary: The Dental Sleep Assistant is responsible for delivering an ideal patient experience and an optimal appointment through efficient and effective assisting of dentists with patient care. This includes operatory preparation and sterilization, device handling, and administrative EMR documentation. Acquiring necessary patient records, lab case submission, and ongoing patient engagement also fall within the purview of this critical role.

Although daily responsibilities may vary in our dynamic environment, the Dental Sleep Assistant will always be responsible for the following tasks:

- **Patient Engagement**
  - Greet patients with sincere warmth.
  - Provide patients with relevant information regarding their appointment
  - Consult with patient and accurately document relevant notes in EMR
  - Answer questions
  - Schedule next appointment
- **Clinical Functions**
  - Take accurate dental impressions using digital and analog methods
  - Detail differences in form and functionality of commonly used appliances
  - Troubleshoot device issues with dentists and make necessary adjustments
  - Prepare, sterilize, and maintain operatories for patient visits
  - Order, ship, check-in, and maintain lab cases
  - Update relevant notes in EMR
  - Coordinate with sleep lab, HST company, and referring sleep physicians for sleep testing information
  - Distribute, document, and maintain home sleep testing program
- **Team Development**
  - Participate in regularly scheduled team meetings
  - Relay relevant details regarding supply ordering
  - Continue education through online learning, journals, and live events
  - Interact with colleagues in a professional, personable manner
  - Assist with all other functions as needed

DETAILED COMPENSATION OVERVIEW
This is a full-time, salaried position demanding a minimum of 36 hours per week. Transform Dental Sleep will provide an annual base salary of $XX,000. Production and collections incentive opportunities are available which will make you eligible for approximately $X,000 in additional compensation. Company medical insurance benefits are available after $$$XX days of employment, and a 401(k) program with limited company match is available after 1 year of employment.

HIRING

Pairing the right person with the right role can be a colossal challenge. The wrong person can mean costly setbacks, with explicit costs for training, scrubs, and more. The implicit costs are even greater; you still don't have someone to do the job, and the rest of the team is encumbered with the extra workload.

Earlier in this section, you read about charging your imagination when looking for prospective team members. Sometimes you can find them online or through staffing firms. If you choose to run an ad online, make it as unique as your practice. A drab, cookie-cutter ad will appeal to drab, cookie-cutter applicants. Several people have told me that they applied for a job I posted because they found the ad compelling. Don't be afraid to grab people's attention. It'll turn off the unenthusiastic job seekers and attract people with the "it" factor. Write it yourself, call me, use ChatGPT … just make it happen.

As described earlier, you can also find great candidates in the wild. Even if you've encouraged your favorite barista to apply or submit a resume, they'll still have to undergo a vetting and formal interview process.

Many interviews are reminiscent of the Chris Farley Show skit on *Saturday Night Live* back in the day. Chris interviewed celebrities in a one-on-one format. He'd play a nervous, fawning fan while conversing with huge celebrities, then beat himself up when he made a faux pas. Speaking with Paul McCartney, for example, he'd say, "R-r-remember when you were with The Beatles?" McCartney answers affirmatively. Then Farley rebounds with, "That was awesome," to which Sir Paul answers, "Yes it was." Then Chris follows up with a question regarding rumors that Paul McCartney had died, asking, "That was a hoax, right?"

He was sitting next to McCartney, asking him that question. Finally, Farley self-flagellates, saying "I'm so *stupid.*"

This isn't far from what goes down in a lot of interviews. Typically, the office manager scans the applicant's resume and says, "It says here you worked at Dr. Green's office for about two years." "Yes." "And it looks like you used Dentrix there and Eaglesoft when you worked at Dr. Magnuson's office." "Yes." "How'd you like working there?" "It was pretty good."

While Chris Farley would actually physically hit himself in the head for asking a dumb question, you beat yourself up figuratively after you realize that you hired a pet rock instead of a front-office dynamo. The interview process is often seen as a technicality or an opportunity to see if you'll "get along" with the candidate while reviewing the collection of half-truths and platitudes known as a resume.

Practice Marketing Coordinator Sample Ad

This is an incredibly dynamic, extremely rewarding position but only for the right person. We aren't desperate, and we won't hire just anyone. We want to ensure we're a great fit for you and your career path. Naturally, we also want to be certain you're a good fit for our team and our patients.

Our practice provides life-saving sleep apnea treatment to patients in need of an alternative to CPAP therapy. Millions of people would benefit from this therapy if they simply knew about it. We are seeking a multi-hat wearing, multi-skill developing, crazy passionate, dedicated lifelong learner to work alongside us as a Marketing Coordinator.

Below are some things that are *NOT* required:

☐ College graduate   ☐ Proficiency in rocket science

☐ Expert-level experience in marketing   ☐ Ninjitsu skills

You do *NOT* have to know anything about dentistry or sleep apnea today. You do have to be a committed learner that is eager to learn new skills, develop existing skills, and rise to new heights. That's what we do today. Every day.

What are you doing today? Are you stagnant? Underwhelmed? Under-challenged? Underpaid?

Then, let us tell you more about *IS REQUIRED* for this uniquely rewarding opportunity:

☐ Exceptionally strong written and verbal communication skills

☐ 7/10 level of graphic design skill using Adobe Creative Suite

☐ Social media marketing experience using HootSuite or similar platform

☐ Self-driven critical thinking skills

☐ Familiarity with Google Suite, e.g calendar, Google Docs, Sheets, etc.

If we select each other for this position, you will collaborate with our Marketing Director to develop new patient outreach campaigns, patient referral programs, and drive physician meeting initiatives. Various administrative responsibilities will also be required such as ordering collateral, inputting CRM data, scheduling practice travel, and more.

You might be thinking, "Well, that all sounds great, but what's in it for me?" Glad you asked. Keep reading:

⇒ Salary ranging from X to Y depending on experience
⇒ Blah Blah Blah Benefits
⇒ No weekends
⇒ Growth potential
⇒ Basically, the coolest career ever

If you've ever said, 'But, that's not my job', then this isn't for you. Not every day is a party, but if you are ready to step into an energetic, non-corporate, "work family" environment, then we want to meet you! You'll learn a ton, earn a ton, and change lives – including your own.

A purposeful interview takes more time and effort on the front end, but it'll save you tons of time, money, and hassle in the long run. I've hired around 100 people in various businesses over the years and more than 90 of them were "winner, winner, falafel dinner." You know some of these people and count them among your favorites in the industry. Lemme provide you a few tips based on my experience. Take what you want and leave the rest.

Four ears are better than two. Always interview with at least one other person present, usually the office manager or sleep champion. One of you might pick up on something the other missed. Oftentimes, I'll try to interview with two other people—one with a high degree of technical knowledge regarding the tasks the prospective employee will perform, and the other should be someone who will manage or work with this person routinely. They'll have their own take on whether the candidate is a good fit.

Review the resume in advance and get the other interviewers to review it, too. What stands out about their experience, and how might it apply to your open position? Note any areas where you really want to drill deeper.

Kick off the interview by explaining what you're doing and why you're doing it this way. Remember, most people are accustomed to routine interviews. For example, you can say, "Thanks for coming in today. Our purpose is to get to know more about you and your goals while sharing salient details about who we are and what we need. Then we can decide whether we can help each other reach our goals together. Let's just have an open dialogue. You'll see us jotting down some notes here. Don't worry, it doesn't mean anything negative. We're just trying to keep everything straight. We'll ask a lot of questions because we really want to get to know you, and we want you to know us. We follow the 80/20 rule around here. We want you to love working here 80 percent of the time, and we'll be ecstatic that you're here 80 percent of the time. We're all human and have some 'off' days. We're looking for someone who will make our practice their home. Sound good?" This should set them at ease.

Use exploratory questions from the R.E.A.D. section of this book to assess the experiences of the front-office candidate who used Dentrix and Eaglesoft. Which system did they find more intuitive to use? On a scale of 1-10, how difficult was it to switch from one to the other? What type of training did they receive? What was good about the training and what was lacking? Questions like these will elicit answers that tell you what they need to know if you're listening.

If your candidate responds that one system was much easier to use than the other, you can compare that with your own experience. Based on the ranking response, you can surmise how technically proficient someone is and their amenability to change. Their answers to the training questions will help you determine whether the person is a self-starter or needs to be spoon-fed.

People will over-share when given an opportunity to speak openly. When asked what was good about their training and what was deficient, many people will seize the opportunity to vent about what they didn't like. Pay attention here. Do their veins in their neck bulge out while they're recounting the experience? Do they pound the table and turn into The Hulk? During an interview, they're showing you their essential selves. Now, imagine four months from now, when you announce that you're switching from one EMR to another and how they're going to respond.

At the interview's conclusion, share clearly what the next steps will be. "Thanks for coming in today. We're going to speak with a few other people and aim to decide by next Friday. Whichever way it goes, you'll hear from us by Friday. Thanks so much for coming in to chat with us."

After they leave, download immediately with your fellow interviewers and compare notes. Did the candidate arrive a few minutes early? Was their appearance appropriate? Did they present themselves such that you'd be proud to have them represent your business? Can you picture them doing the job tomorrow? What about in two years? What were the other panelists' impressions? Maybe you didn't notice that she was chewing gum and had a culturally insensitive tattoo. Perhaps her responses to the technical questions unearthed how outdated her experience was.

To hire or not to hire? That *is* the question. Together, you can make a more informed decision.

FOUR Es TO RETAIN TOP TALENT

"Take care of the people, the products, and the profits – in that order."
—Jim Barksdale

You have a vision and an outline, but you cannot do it alone. Many have tried. All have failed. One of the attractions of oral appliance therapy is that it's largely a team driven procedure, and yet most DSM wannabes don't invest in their teams. Instead, they attend annual meetings singing the blues about how bad their teams suck and refuse to get on board. Everything you've read here thus far is intended to help you overcome these kinds of issues. Now you have to delegate. The only way you'll succeed in this journey is with a smooth-functioning team.

That doesn't mean you should simply dump all the stuff you don't want to do or don't have time to do on your team's shoulders. That's a recipe for turnover. Lots of turnover. It also doesn't mean you should micro-manage them to death. That's a blueprint for calamity. Delegating doesn't mean barking orders or passive aggressively ordering your office manager to issue dictates.

We're going to review what effective delegation *does* entail. We'll define the roles, map the processes to match the right roles with the right people, and then review efficacious techniques so your team can go forth and prosper. No bio-gunk will be absorbed in the following pages; just the stuff you need.

Direct reports often fail to meet expectations because they're not clear about where they're going, what they're supposed to be doing, or how their success will be measured. Oftentimes, they lack the education, authority, and/or resources necessary to do what needs to be done.

Let's front-flip from the theoretical to the practical with the "4 Es." This is where the rubber meets the road so you can delegate like a champ. The 4 Es position you to cultivate and keep top talent. Following these principles will give your team a sense of ownership, set them up to outperform your wildest expectations, and lessen your mental and physical loads.

1. **EDUCATE:** Give your team the information they need to do their jobs confidently and competently. There are scores of ways to do this; from online learning management systems and live CE events to sponsored bootcamps and onsite training. You have options.

   Don't simply sign the team up for an event and tell them they're going. That's a wasted opportunity. Harness the communication techniques we've covered previously to explain the purpose, process, and anticipated payoff from the educational sessions.

   Consider something like this: "I registered the team for a medical billing course at a hotel downtown on the 15th of next month. That's typically our admin day. The company hosting it is the one that does our medical billing and provides our software, too. Of course, you'll be paid for the entire day. I'm hoping you can learn more about the software and what hacks are available to make our processes easier and get claims paid faster. By the end of the event, I expect you'll get all your questions cleared up, you'll have a better relationship with their team, and working with them will be easier."

   You'll continue to build your knowledge base, and your team should, too. Don't just send them to one course or one webinar. Learn together. Keep learning. Don't stop. Ever.

2. **EQUIP:** Give them the tools and resources they need to do the work. You're cognizant of costs. Because mindfulness of your bottom line is crucial to run a successful practice, frugality is your friend. However, your team needs functioning computers. I once worked at a place that spent $1,000 in labor to avoid spending $250 on a new hard drive.

   Don't expect your team to track your patients' progress adequately and accurately with a pirated Excel sheet. Buck up for a Microsoft Office subscription so they'll have full functionality. Better yet, use Google Sheets. on second thought, subscribe to a dedicated DSM EMR.

   A digital scanner isn't an absolute necessity, but after some training, your remakes will go down, turnaround times will decrease, patients will be happier, and your team will be, too. These are just a few suggestions to save them time, which saves you money. It'll also make their tasks easier, which will make your life better. Equip them with the tools they need to do the job effectively and efficiently.

3. **EMPOWER:** Give them autonomy. Your team must have the freedom to make decisions, make magic and, sometimes, make mistakes. They need to feel safe to learn, question, experiment, and grow without fear of being fired.

   The onus is on you to install sensible guardrails, e.g., "Here's a canvas and some paint. You can actually use whatever you want from this art drawer, but it has to fit on this canvas, and everything has to be clean when you're finished."

   You're not micromanaging the team or the processes which is a surefire way to stifle creativity, hinder learning, crush morale, and heighten anxiety. Give them the space to create and execute.

I mentioned previously that in a past professional life, I managed a software company. We had just one hard rule: no customer was given the service for free. Everything else was in play, providing plenty of teachable moments. We had a couple of sales reps, and one consistently outperformed the other despite having similar opportunities. After sitting in and listening to five of the underperformer's calls, I asked her what she would do differently. She identified the same issues: missed opportunities to close the sale and a propensity to keep talking, overly justifying the price. I empathized with her, and we role-played different approaches to similar situations. She got better fast.

If you want to empower your team, give them no-go boundaries, and grant permission to screw up. When they do—and they will— sit with them and explore why they did what they did. What was their rationale? Then suggest different ways they might deal with similar situations in the future. Describe how this solution will lead to more desirable results. Connect the dots and state your expectation that they'll adopt this new-and-improved method in the future. If you don't do this and things don't work out, it's on you.

Avoid making your team feel like cogs in a machine by micromanaging them. This can happen when you feel out of the loop. You don't need to know every step of every process. You have your own issues to focus on. They can give you high-level updates during team meetings. When your team flexes their autonomy, you'll begin to see exponential growth.

4. **ENCOURAGE:** Give your team constructive feedback and praise them for their progress. Reward victory and strive to convert misses into learning opportunities and future wins. I'm not talking about, "everybody gets a trophy" type of praise. Coddling is counter-

productive. Tie appropriate commendations to specific behaviors. Don't overlook opportunities to encourage because you're "too busy."

Example: "Steve, I heard the way you coached Mrs. Doubtfire to wear her morning aligner while doing her household chores. That was really great listening and a great suggestion."

Another example: "We got our first three referrals from Dr. Oatdontwurk, Angela. I know how challenging it was to help him understand that appliance therapy works for many patients. Great job. Your persistence really paid off. What do you think it was that finally nudged him to send not just one patient but three, your freakin' superstar?"

Say what you mean and mean what you say. Speak directly but kindly. Don't be brusque. Be professional. Provide the tools to do the job, space to make mistakes, coaching to correct, and clear benchmarks for success. It won't drain your hourglass. Nor will it zap your energy. It might test your patience, but if done right, proper delegation converts your team into a renewable resource.

It doesn't cost anything except you paying attention. Everyone can afford it. The payoff is sizable when considering the time savings, morale boost, and productivity gains. 4 Es. You're making moves and making things happen. The verdict is in. It's time to execute.

W.O.W. ERIN ELLIOTT

Author's note: Dr. Erin Elliott has presented all over the country spreading the dental sleep medicine gospel. Many of her lectures focus on the practical aspects of sleep implementation within a busy general dentistry practice. She definitely walks her talk – bouncing between restorative patients and sleep patients in her busy Post Falls Family Dental and Sleep Better Northwest practices. I'm thankful to count E3 as a friend. —Jason Tierney

I'm a dentist, a general dentist to be exact. I don't do sleep full-time—there are too many patients who need fillings, crowns, and extractions.

Some say it's not possible to do both. Dejected, others moan "It's just too hard." Well, I'm here to tell you that if I can do it, anybody can do it. My secret weapon, my secret sauce, my ace in the hole? MY TEAM!

Ask yourself, "What exactly does the doctor *have* to do by law?" Or, "What exactly does the doctor *have* to do for the best patient care?" In my world the answer is, the consult. That's the time when I help connect the dots for the patient on how their sleep apnea probably affects their life more than they think—things like bruxing, acid reflux, and nocturia—and it's when I evaluate their airway and anatomy and joint for suitability and type of oral appliance. That's it. And most of that's already been done by my sleep apnea coordinator.

Sleep apnea coordinator, you say? Yes, a sleep apnea coordinator. For a smaller team, it might not be possible to have a team member dedicated entirely to your sleep program. It's easy to say you can't have a full-time team member dedicated to sleep because you don't have enough sleep patients. How can you create the need for a sleep coordinator without a sleep coordinator? Listen to me: You. Need. To. Create. The. Need.

Think of sleep as a separate business in your practice. Give it a startup investment, hire from within, promote a team member to sleep coordinator, and give them the time. Give them six months to make it happen. If they don't have patients, no problem. You can screen your team members, their families, and your hygiene patients.

They can look at tomorrow's charts and find patients on high blood pressure or diabetes meds. Find patients with clinical signs of bruxing or who've had a night guard previously.

Collect medical insurance cards at the front desk and learn how to do eligibility checks so you can estimate their out-of-pocket cost based on their medical insurance while they're still in the chair. If they don't have patients, then they have time to go out and build relationships with medical providers, athletic trainers, dieticians, chiropractors, optometrists, and other potential referral sources. Get creative.

Finally, they'll have time to build a social media presence, film testimonials, and bring the message directly to the consumer through emotional stories that each patient type and demographic can identify with.

I'm a straight shooter. You may not like directness, but I am here to tell you two mantras in my life. *#makeithappen* and *#FIOS* (Figure It Out Stupid—or Silly—depending on the audience). There are no excuses, and if you don't like your situation, *change it*. Sleep medicine can be done in a general dental office. In fact, sleep must be done for our general dental patients. Sleep in your general dental office will grow to the point that your practice stands apart from every other office.

Take the risk. Take charge, invest your time and money, and maybe, just maybe, you have to be willing to sacrifice your favorite chairside assistant or hygienist by giving them an opportunity to make a career rather than take a job. They'll stay with you and your patients' lives will improve one night at a time while your practice changes one day at a time.

FIG 16 "EXECUTE"

EXECUTE *VERB*

1: to carry out fully: put completely into effect

2: to do what is provided or required by

3: to make or produce (something, such as a work of art) especially by carrying out a design

"Doubt is removed by action." —Conor McGregor

Dental sleep conferences always conjure up an anecdote told by billionaire investor Charlie Munger, regarding the composer Wolfgang Amadeus Mozart:

A young man came to Mozart and said, "I want to compose symphonies. I want to talk to you about that."

Mozart said, "How old are you?"

"Twenty-two."

"You're too young to do symphonies," Mozart said.

"But you were writing symphonies when you were ten years old."

"Yes, but I wasn't running around asking other people how to do it."

Mic drop.

I shouldn't tell you this, but we make fun of you. At the big sleep conferences, all the vendors trade stories and make up nicknames for you. Maybe not you specifically, but a composite, made up of your cohort of quagmires. The benign barbs frequently focus on dentists' claims that they're at an inflection point to revolutionize DSM despite treating few, if any, patients. Oh, and they'll send business to the sales reps turned comedians, provided they give a steep volume discount, but for now they just want everything free.

"Tell you what, Dr. Doolittle, I'll give you a discount on an HST unit when you buy one. You've been asking me for a discount for the past four years. I loaned you a unit for a month, and you never tested a single patient. Not one."

"Oh yeah, reminds me of Dr. Ima Theenkabotit. She comes by our booth and asks a thousand questions. Then she's like, 'Can you come by my office to discuss how I can transition to DSM only?' I say, 'how about starting with treating one patient? Just one. *Not two. Just one!*'"

"Next level. I'm gonna be in seven physicians' offices. You guys are gonna have to step up your manufacturing capacities to keep up with all my cases."
"Whatever, Doc. Let's start with sending, you know, one case per month."

The newer vendors still have moon-shot aspirations. They see the problems as opportunities, and they want to help. They're not wrong. Vast possibilities exist for dentists to help patients with sleep issues.

Those who've been around the block, though, we're a different story. Once I was chopping it up with a vendor who's also a dentist. A dental duo approached me who'd been attending meetings for a long time without much action or traction. Like a ventriloquist, through a forced smile, Dr. Vendor gritted, "One has the warmth of the Arctic Circle, and the other acts like he got punched in the head too many times."

Most of the sidebars recount past run-ins with dentists and their hollow plans to kickstart a new DSM program. Episodic brain-drain sessions punctuate spans of predictable post-meeting ghosting. That's what we find most confounding. If you say, "Sure, I'll fill out your form and get in your marketing funnel to learn about your products," but then never engage further, that's cool. It happens. You feigned interest or had a modicum of actual curiosity that waned. No biggie. It's the sporadic calls and texts afterward with detailed what-would-you-do scenarios and whataboutisms, and "I heard from a guy at the 'Society of Sleep Weirdos' meeting that if we don't store our bites in a shoe box with four physician signatures when treating Aetna patients, we'll go to jail unless we buy her stay-out-of-jail documents." That's what baffles us.

These calls become color commentary for jokes at the next meeting. They also pull back the curtain, revealing sleep dentistry's most glaring deficiency: an aversion to action. Dentists call home sleep test service providers and medical billing companies, but never contract business. Those dentists don't need to take more classes; they need to take more action.

We're all familiar with analysis paralysis. We analyze, over-analyze, then re-over-analyze. Again. This crippling, fear-centric behavior is prevalent among dental sleep practitioners. Their intentions are good, but their actions fall short. They sit on the sidelines, Monday morning quarterbacking the discussion away. There's always a new anecdote or an article that's a cause for pause. If not that, it's some practice or personal affair that impedes action. Once that's resolved, *then* they'll start screening patients, *then* they'll begin reaching out to physicians, *then* they'll begin a training program for their team.

"Which appliance is best?"

"Which billing company should I use if I'm out-of-network, but there's an in-network physician two towns over and his son is an exceptional hockey player?"

Well-meaning dentists ask these questions of every single appliance manufacturer and every billing company at the meeting. They'll take sample appliances, product literature, and time. They want it all. Months later, they'll call other vendors and ask the same questions.

Then, equipped with all this cutting-edge information, these dentists table DSM implementation until they ... learn more. Whatever that means. They're so concerned about the anecdote some dentist from a different state said he heard from a golf buddy about some other dentists who were getting sued for treating sleep. Meanwhile, the dentist across the hall read an article two weeks ago about snoring and sleep apnea, saw a ProSomnus ad last week, and she's already taking scans for her third precision medical device. Good for her. Great for her patients.

I'm not dissing you from my glass house. I've certainly succumbed to the dreaded analysis paralysis. When I first started running on trails, I considered purchasing a pair of shoes specifically designed for this type of running. I ruminated about whether I actually needed them. Then I asked a couple people who ran trails. They recommended the shoes highly. I followed up with some research online, then read more articles, product comparisons, and varying views on what criteria really matter when purchasing trail shoes. Eventually I made it to the running store, asked some questions, and tried on a couple of pairs.

Then I went home empty handed. Two weeks later, I finally bought a pair of shoes. I ran in them and didn't lose footing, slip down descents, or crumple when I banged my toe against boulders. The shoes made my runs much better, but it was still just running. It wasn't that different from what I'd been doing. If I could do it over, I wouldn't have wasted three weeks pondering every inane detail about toe drops and water resistance levels. I would have spent the time running trails.

Loaded question: Which appliance is best?

Simple answer: The precision medical device that's best for the patient and they'll actually wear most nights.

That's it. Are some better than others? Sure—if your patient was confined to a closet for 16 years and is now claustrophobic, a TAP device probably isn't the way to go. Someone in your chair with lowers they've bruxed into nubs? Skip an EMA on that one. That first patient would probably do just fine with an EMA and the second would likely do well with a TAP device. Learn. Do. Repeat. Don't stop at the first step. Nike sums it up in three words, "Just Do It." Start here and now.

In his brilliant *War of Art*, Steven Pressfield anthropomorphizes this reluctance to act as The Resistance. He deftly describes situations we've all encountered and presents actionable steps to overcome sleep-practice-killing resistance. You can frame your caution as due diligence, and it probably started out that way, but don't analyze until the opportunity has passed or you've snuffed out any meaningful momentum.

In 1933, psychologist Carl Jung replied to a letter from someone inquiring about how to live a good life. His thoughtful response: "Your questions are unanswerable because you want to know how one *ought* to live. One lives as one *can*. There is no single, definite way for the individual which is prescribed for him or would be the proper one...But if you want to go your individual way, it is the way you make for yourself, which is never prescribed, which you do not know in advance, and which simply comes into being of itself when you put one foot in front of the other."

Even though it's called a "practice," we can't treat it like a perpetual dress rehearsal. Learn from your colleagues. Gather information from vendors. Then execute. No practitioner has everything figured out. We learn. We act. We grow.

W.O.W. JEFF RODGERS

Author's note: Dr. Jeff Rodgers was like many of the dentists described here. Then something changed. He changed. From his physical fitness to the immense growth he's experienced in his practice, Sleep Better Georgia, he is a living testament to the rewards of executing habitually on one's commitments. —Jason Tierney

My life didn't please me, so I created my life." —Coco Chanel

I have a saying that sits on my desk as a constant reminder of where I was and where I want to be. It simply reads: "Don't be a dead squirrel." Squirrels are certainly quick enough to escape oncoming traffic, but only if they choose one path, i.e., get the hell out of the path of oncoming vehicles. If they freeze in fear, they're not going to live to eat another acorn. I should know. I used to be a dead squirrel, languishing in the middle of the road doing nothing and suffering from analysis paralysis. I failed to act because of my fear over what could go wrong.

My internal dialogue was constant and exhausting, sounding something like this:

Should I buy stock in that widget company? What if it goes down? What if it goes up?

Should I hire that extra employee? What if revenue doesn't go up?

Should I treat this patient for OSA even though they may need some dental work? Will they be upset if their appliance needs to be remade?

I didn't know it at the time, but I was living out of a scarcity mentality, and I was trapped in the small world I had created for myself. Thanks to some traumatic life events and the help of an outstanding counselor, I had a conversion at the core of my being. I learned to recognize the mental, emotional, and relational cost of living in fear and staying small. The office was stagnant, my number of friendships was small, and I never moved forward. So, I changed. Dramatically.

My circle of friends changed. My personal life changed. My office changed. My body changed. Even the car I drive changed.

Don't get me wrong; this kind of change is really hard, and I can't tell you how many times I was wracked with even more fear over the changes I was trying to make. I was being told that this path would lead to a better life, but I didn't experientially know it yet. Luckily, that too, changed quickly.

The fear doesn't go away completely; it's still there sometimes, but it no longer rules my life or hijacks my internal monologue. It's simply a reflexive instinct, left over from some old beliefs that I've learned to work through. Now those thoughts are less like roadblocks in my way and more like clouds that float through my mind while I press on to bigger and better things.

If you suffer from "analysis paralysis," I encourage you to look closely at what it's costing you and how it benefits you. After all, you get to create your own life. It takes courage to work on yourself and take big, bold steps, but it's a fun road to be on when you're not stuck in the rut of your own fear. I'm still on the journey—and it is a journey, not a destination—but I know that there's no way I'm ever going back.

Start working on yourself. I'll be here on this road with you, and there are lots of other people out there who want you to think big, live big, LOVE BIG. Here's the thing: when you consciously create your own life, you inspire others to do the same.

ARE YOU QUALIFIED?

"Where do you start? You start right here. When do you start? You start right now. You initiate action. You go." —Jocko Willink

Prior to the AADSM's Mastery programs, earning Diplomate status with the American Board of Dental Sleep Medicine (ABDSM) was an arduous task, involving exhaustive documentation of completed cases that fell within narrow parameters, hours logged observing overnight at a sleep lab, letters of recommendation from sleep physicians, didactic courses, the exam, and oh so much more. It was overkill. Because of this gauntlet, only a few hundred dentists across the U.S. earned the coveted status.

That's all changed. The AADSM's presumably benevolent attempts to increase patient access to dental sleep medicine solutions have led them to ease the guidelines, inflating the number of Diplomates. Now, earning one of these professional designations mandates that dentists attend didactic training courses and pass an exam. No demonstration of clinical competency is required. Like your first job at McDonald's, no actual experience is needed.

Now there are more ABDSM Diplomates than ever before. Many of them have literally never *ever* treated a patient with oral appliance therapy. Add the other pop-up organizations that claim to credential dentists and you've got the DSM version of the wild west. One organization says *this*. The other says *that*. And they're all filling their coffers. I've talked with some of the dentists who've completed these programs. OAT is still an abstraction to many of them. They're like, "So, I got my Diplomate. Now what do I do?"

Paradoxically, a wealth of DSM education can lead to a poverty of treated patients. I'm not decrying the value of education, but the application of knowledge matters. As Stephen King wrote about writing, "It is, after all, the dab of grit that seeps into an oyster's shell that makes the pearl, not the pearl-making seminars with other oysters."

You have to screen patients. You have to engage your team. You have to prescribe and deliver appliances. You must execute. Only then will you become proficient and prolific. You cannot learn your way to dental sleep medicine success. You have to *do* it.

GET READY, GET S.E.T.T., AND GO!

"Whatever you can do, or dream you can, begin it. Boldness has genius, magic, and power in it. Begin it now." —*Johann Wolfgang von Goethe*

Love 'em or hate 'em: acronyms can be a highly effective mnemonic devices helping to commit ideas and processes to memory. S.E.T.T. stands for Screen, Engage, Test, and Treat. Get to the starting line, get S.E.T.T. and go. This is a rallying cry, a battle hymn. You can't read this book and just think about it. You must make a choice and act. Stop thinking about who you could be or what you should be and transform into what you are.

Screen your patients

Don't take it from me. The American Dental Association and the American Academy of Dental Sleep Medicine both recommend that dentists screen their patients for sleep-related breathing disorders. Seldom do patients stroll into the dentist's office and plead for oral appliance therapy.

A low-friction, replicable screening protocol is paramount. Period. A good friend owned a medical billing company. Hundreds of dentists signed up for their DSM billing services. After their onboarding service reps contacted a practice innumerable times for onboarding—to no avail—the dentist would inevitably call the office and demand that all monies be refunded.

Their reason? "It didn't work, and we didn't get paid."

"Tell me more, Doctor Dick."

"None of my patients wanted to do this, and you never trained my team. I want my money back. And don't even think about denying me. I'm very influential in the ADA."

Most of the time, my friend just told them to get lost. Envious of her moxie, I wish I could've mustered the same fearlessness when dealing with Dr. Dumass back in the day. With the others, she'd mention the 17 times her colleagues emailed, called, and left messages to schedule billing training. She'd offer to play recordings of the team talking to his staff and being told they don't want to be trained. Then she reminded him that he never actually submitted a claim. He admitted that was because he never actually got around to screening patients.

You have to actually screen your patients if you're going to eventually get compensated for treating patients. If you don't want to treat patients or get involved with DSM, there's no law that says you have to. You can do whatever you want but make your choice. Don't make a half-hearted attempt and then scapegoat your billing company. Like *The Big Book* of Alcoholics Anonymous says, "It works if you work it."

Engage your patients

Engaging patients is different from making small talk or telling them what you see on the pano. Engage means connecting. Developing trust. Giving and taking.

Communication underpins engagement, case acceptance, and patient loyalty. It is in the DNA of successful sales processes too. The entire previous chapter was a love song to this concept. Go back and reread it if you need to. Relate to your patients and explore what their needs are. Advise workable solutions and deliver on your promises. Talk to them like human beings and show them you care.

Test your patients

There's more than one way to do this, and the rationale is 20/20. Treating a patient without a proper diagnosis is never a good idea. As a matter of fact, it's a terrible idea.

With that out of the way, should you purchase and dispense your own home sleep testing units? Or should you use a home sleep testing service to manage the process? Instead, what if you refer your patients to a sleep doc? The answer to those questions is simply "yes." Depending on your practice's situation, these might all be viable solutions. A hybrid is probably your best bet. Purchase several units for titration studies. Develop bilateral referral relationships with numerous physicians. Take advantage of a third-party HST service. Medicare guidelines, insurance plans, state dental practice acts all need to be considered.

Converse with a couple vendors. They're exposed to more testing models in a single week than you'll see in your entire career. They're a fount of information. Ask a couple successful DSM practitioners how they do it. Then take this information and take action.

Treat your patients

This is the easy one. It's in your wheelhouse. Look at the patient's unique presentation, consider appliance selection criteria, and take accurate records. Follow up appropriately. Easy-peasy. Don't over-complicate this one.

Maybe you're thinking, "But, Jason, I don't have any patients yet." That's nonsense. Start with your team and their spouses. It's that simple. The best learning comes from doing.

IF IT DOESN'T MAKE DOLLARS, IT DOESN'T MAKE SENSE

Earlier, I shared that I once worked at a dental lab that manufactured oral appliances. Like a Bill Murray-less *Groundhog Day*, the customer service team called dentists every day to get feedback about their first cases. Dentists exalted about how the patient's spouse thanked them with hugs, cookies, or the whole Sentimental Value Meal. "It was the easiest thing I've done as a dentist, and they were both so damn happy. By the way, what do other dentists normally charge for these things?"

"It varies, but it's usually between $3,000 and $6,000," the rep would answer.

"WHAT?! Are you kidding me? That seems criminal. I just doubled the lab fee. You're telling me that dentists are charging $6,000 for these, seriously?" From benevolent DDS to greedy SOB; the transformation was complete.

The rep continued, "You'll have to bill medical insurance, not dental insurance, to see those kinds of numbers, plus a copy of the patient's sleep study and some other documentation. Inside the case box, there were some basic tips for medical billing, codes, and contact info for a couple of exceptional billing companies that focus on this stuff."

Click! Dr. McGreedy would hang up at this point and pull his office manager into the room. "You know that snore appliance we just delivered? We could've gotten six grand for it from his medical insurance. Go dig the box out of the trash and let's bill insurance next time we do one. I want to start doing more of these things."

"OK, what information do they need? Do they need a pano? You sure I can't just send it to Delta?

The office manager, Mrs. Dumass-McGreedy submits claims for the next three cases. On the first, they receive payment for $5,789. They do happy dances around the break room. The results are not so great for the other two cases. Even though they filled out the forms just like in the webinar, one claim is denied, and the other only pays $826.

What in the ever-loving fudge happened? She navigated the nine levels of voice prompt hell, only to end up in "transfer you to another representative" purgatory. After repeatedly recounting all the details to each human when they actually picked up the phone, she's *finito*.

The denial probably had something to do with Dr. McGreedy's multiple personalities as the ordering physician for the sleep test and the prescribing doctor for the device. Cutting corners in the name of greed is a losing proposition for all parties. Doc doesn't get the production and is jeopardizing his livelihood, and the patient fails to get the necessary treatment.

In the span of one presidential term, dentists who'd been floored by the allure of $2,000 checks were now complaining about the occasional $1,400 Medicare allowable that fell between their $6,000 Plan F and Plan G patients. Cries of, "It's just not worth it anymore" could be heard from rapacious lecturers. Scurrilous billing companies popped up, pushing dodgy billing protocols. I attended a course in California where the speaker displayed slides showing EOBs for $19,000. Stories like these spread quickly through the grapevine, and suddenly $2,000 for an hour of doctor time and a life saved isn't worth the squeeze. The zeitgeist changed fast. This is a problem for patients, practices, and the profession.

Smart dentists treating 1–30 patients per month outsource their medical billing to a third-party service. Like restaurants, running shoes, and real estate, not all medical billing companies are created equal. Most of them—not all, but most—will do a decent job submitting your claims and working them for you.

Many billing companies bill you a percentage of what the claim pays. The more you make, the more they make. Theoretically, this incentivizes them to maximize the amount collected for you. The best companies provide you with a pristine EMR to seamlessly submit documents for processing.

The greatest distinction between companies is the levels of communication and support. Communication is a differentiator. Peter Thiel's quote in a previous section is especially resonant, "Superior sales and distribution by itself can create a monopoly, even with no product differentiation."

Don't do the billing company bop. If you're getting reimbursement for most cases and your team is generally happy with the billing company's communication, then stay with that company. If you don't get paid for a claim or the allowable is less than you're accustomed to, ask your billing company for details. Don't disparage them on social media or denigrate them while you call their competitors. There are as many different insurance plans as you have hairs on your head. Each plan has their own sinister American Ninja Warrior obstacle course to navigate, and they often add new hoops, twists, and turns without warning. The better billing companies stay abreast of these changes, allowing them to navigate the course as best as it can be. Still, it's a rigged game. If you're working with the best third parties, they'll figure things out for you and keep you updated. If your company isn't doing that for you, then, yeah, it's time to find a new one.

I know a few practices that treat more than 120 patients every month, earning millions and bettering the health and well-being of entire zip codes. Most of The 100 Club's elite prescribe different devices. Some of their practices are entirely physician referral-based, while others focus on direct-to-patient marketing. Nearly all of these practitioners rely on a hybrid sleep testing model, but not all of them do. Each practice is as different as Mars and Venus.

Despite their myriad differences, though, their similarities are more important. Each practice invests in their teams. They hire well, they train well, and they give their team members the four Es. They hold their teams accountable, they communicate effectively, and they execute.

What's stopping you from joining The 100 Club? You know what you need to do. It's all right here in black and white. Like interest, success compounds. One patient becomes two, and two become four. If you're still having doubts about your ability to execute, just heed my mom's advice: "Make it happen."

W.O.W. RANDY CURRAN

Author's note: Medical billing for oral appliance therapy is a study in contrasts. There are requirements and exceptions; guidelines and exemptions; guidance and loopholes. It's all in black and white, and yet it's all a mystery. Thank heavens for Randy Curran, co-founder and CEO of Pristine Medical Billing. He's the oracle of medical billing. He's brash, bald, and ultra-knowledgeable about DSM billing. Randy loves baseball, his family, and his team. I'm grateful to have him as my go-to subject matter expert.

—Jason Tierney

Throughout my 12-year dental sleep medicine journey, I've learned a lot about medical insurance coverage criteria regarding oral appliances, claim pricing, and payment methods. In this time, I've also gotten a considerable education on how dental practices work and the challenges they face in implementing dental sleep medicine programs.

Most dentists come in hot, eager to begin treating their patients. Somehow, somewhere, they've heard through the grapevine that most practices are delivering 20-30 cases within the first two years. In my experience helping more than 1200 practices get into dental sleep medicine, just one or two dentists have accomplished anything like this. Most practices treat 1-3 cases per month in the first year. Exceptional practices might have 3-5 cases during this period. Perhaps by years two and three, they double these figures. There's an unbridgeable chasm separating the unrealistically lofty goals some speakers sell and the reality that dentists buy.

Many dental practices, doing a couple of cases per month, feel they're not succeeding and eventually give up, not realizing that they're on par with 95% of the industry. Treating 2 patients per month means helping 24 people per year live better lives, while also creating safer drivers in your community. This is a major success. Dentists who consistently stay the course and focus on helping more people eventually see those numbers turn into well over 100 patients treated. Accept that the first couple of years will produce 2-4 treated patients per month while you hone your craft and smooth out your processes. What's the alternative? Giving up on dental sleep medicine because you haven't achieved the unrealistically lofty touted by a salesman slinking from town to town?

Besides setting unattainable goals and then beating themselves up for not reaching them, dentists also have to deal with the business of dental sleep medicine. The hardest part of the business side is working with medical insurance carriers to help supplement the cost of treatment. Once the patient understands that this is a medical procedure, they'll want to use their medical insurance to its maximum, given that they pay large premiums for this coverage.

When using medical insurance, the first item that the practice needs to understand is that it's not a panacea. Depending on the time of year, your practice's fee, and the specific medical insurance plan, typically 50-75% of the cost will be covered by insurance. Rarely will it cover the full cost of the treatment, so you need to set accurate expectations upfront with patients. Instead of falsely telling patients, "Yes, your medical insurance will cover this," try a more truthful, "Yes, your medical insurance will cover a portion of this."

Another important element that dental practices must adapt to when using medical insurance is the need to follow the proper steps and workflow to ensure coverage and payment. Many practices jump the gun and deliver the appliance before a pre-authorization is obtained. With medical insurance, a strict workflow must be adhered if you want to succeed consistently. A benefit check must be done to ensure the patient has coverage for a dental sleep medicine device. A pre-authorization is submitted with all of the required clinical records that the particular insurance carrier requires.

A clean, accurate claim is sent, and a proof of delivery must be on file as it might be requested by the carrier.

Don't self-sabotage. Set up a plan and stick to it. Incorporating a pristine workflow takes time. You'll have hiccups. You'll learn. You'll pivot. Stay focused. It's worth it: for your patients, for your practice, your production, and for your community.

FIG 17 "EVALUATE"

EVALUATE *VERB*

1: to determine or fix the value of

2: to determine the significance, worth, or condition of usually by careful appraisal and study

"If a man does not know to what port he is steering, no wind is favorable to him."
—*Seneca*

Without a speedometer, you wouldn't know how fast you're going. Without a scoreboard, you wouldn't know what the score is. Businesses have various KPIs, benchmarks, and metrics. It isn't important what jargon *du jour* you use; what matters is that you establish clear standards so you can track what's working in your practice and what isn't. Armed with this data, you can use the "five whys" technique to analyze why some initiatives succeed and others miss the mark. These markers are indicators of your practice's health.

If you don't know where your destination is, you're guaranteed never to get there. Not all goals are created equal, and goals should be fluid. If you're just getting started, for example, maybe you'll set a goal of two completed cases per month. If you've been treating sleep patients for a while and have been crushing that goal, you shan't do a choreograph a wave around the office every time you do two cases. Instead, you're going to reset the goal. Remember, goals should be specific, measurable, attainable, relevant, and timely.

Is case volume your primary goal? Is it collections per case? What about secondary goals? Patient compliance? Amount of time between receiving a referral to scheduling the patient for a consultation?

What internal metrics should you evaluate? How do you assess your team and determine salary increases, promotions, or hiring and firing needs? Making haphazard decisions based on your gut is not a good idea.

Dr. Nick had a bustling general practice, treating five-to-ten sleep patients each month. He sold the practice and launched a referral-driven, sleep-only office. He follows the R.E.A.D. method and does so many things the right way.

Dr. Nick found out that a dentist on the other side of town, Dr. Perry Meter, was allowed in-network with Plan X, which had previously denied participation for Dr. Nick's practice. Dr. Nick was concerned that lower out-of-pocket costs at Meter's office would override the premium experience he provided at his own practice. So far, his billing team had been successful at obtaining GAP exceptions for patients on Plan X, and most of the time, reimbursement on those cases was bonkers. Still, he demanded that his biller get them enrolled on the plan, too.

After a plethora of politics and hours of phone calls, mission accomplished. Like Dr. Meter's office, now they were also in-network. Within a month, Dr. Nick was back on the warpath.

"Why are we only getting $1,885 for the past two cases we sent to Plan X?" he demanded to know.

"That's our negotiated in-network rate," the biller answered. "Remember when I said ..."

Dr. Nick cut her off, "We used to get four-to-six thousand for those patients' treatment *for the same amount of work! What the ...!*" He stopped and paced, with his hands pressed tightly to his temples. Speaking to himself, the biller, and the DSM gods all at the same time, he exhaled, "Why would we do this? Why would we treat ten patients for $20,000 when we used to treat four patients for the same amount?" The biller reminded

Dr. Nick that he didn't want to potentially lose patients to Dr. Meter due to the in-network discrepancy.

Earlier in the year, Dr. Nick told his team that their goal was to maximize case volume. What he actually wanted was to gradually grow monthly case volume from 40 to 50 patients by the end of the year. This growth rate would allow them to stay in the same space with the same team while he began searching for a second location. He certainly didn't want to backslide, but he didn't want to grow too much, too quickly, either. He definitely didn't want to treat more patients for less, which works against another of his goals: working three-and-a-half days per week since both of his kids are in significant transitional stages, one starting high school, with a full complement of extracurriculars, and the other beginning college. Every additional case means more time at the office. Dr. Nick didn't spell this out for the team, and they aren't mind-readers.

There's a tremendous need for sleep treatment. One in four American adults suffers from OSA. Those patients would have been fine going to Dr. Meter's office. Dr. Nick's superfluous demand to have it all leads to discontent. He's working more for less. And for what? Theodore Roosevelt put the cherry on top with his ditty, "Comparison is the thief of joy."

In lieu of the eleven commandments of sleep success or some other drivel that self-interested companies sell you at their courses, I'll list some benchmarks culled from the scorecards of some of The 100 Club's members, along with metrics they use to evaluate what's working and what needs improvement. Like a buffet or a 12-step meeting, take what you need and leave the rest:

1. **New patient acquisition:** It's important to track new patient stats to evaluate the effectiveness of your marketing efforts, physician networking campaigns, screening protocols, and to identify new growth opportunities.

2. **Treatment acceptance rate:** Here you're monitoring the percentage of patients who accept and proceed with treatment. In a perfect world, the number of patients coming out of the bottom of this funnel mirrors the number going into the top via your screening efforts, physician referrals, external marketing campaigns, and word-of-mouth. A Jarvis Analytics survey showed case acceptance in a general dental practice to be 34 percent, and an informal survey of several 100 Club members revealed numbers closer to 80 percent. Practicing the principles in this book will improve this key metric.

3. **Impressions and deliveries:** Scheduled deliveries are a lagging indicator of the health of your practice. This metric shines a spotlight on your case acceptance prowess, referral generation, and more. If deliveries are down over the previous month, find out why. Are referrals dropping? Is there an increased number of patients that decline treatment? Pay attention to this crucial stat.

4. **Revenue per patient:** We need to evaluate the economic impact of each patient. In your general dentistry practice, you probably use a metric to evaluate the lifetime value of a patient. Are your fees appropriate? Are you billing all the relevant codes to maximize reimbursement? Are your collections processes optimized effectively? Are there additional services you should incorporate for the health of your patients and your practice? Consider myofunctional therapy, nose cones, positional therapy devices, and sleep supplements. Higher revenue per patient means greater profitability.

5. **Billing and collections:** Is your team collecting from patients in a timely manner? Is your billing partner pursuing claims like their livelihood depends on it? What's the average time between claim submission and payment? Are some payors a lot more profitable

than others? Only by evaluating this information can you make informed decisions about how to improve.

6. **Physician referrals:** How many physicians are referring patients? Is there an MD who used to send patients, then stopped? If so, what happened? Did someone recently start sending patients? Where did they come from, and how can you encourage them to send more? Do you have a referral source whose patients seldom convert? This information can help you determine which referral sources need to be contacted, where additional training such as lunch-and-learns might be needed, or when you should hire an external marketing rep.

7. **Screen-to-test ratio:** If you're screening patients in your general practice, how many of those patients agree to proceed with a sleep test? Unlike AHI and RDI, you want this number to be high. If it's below 80 percent, revisit your screening protocols and the script you use to present sleep testing so you can tweak for improvement. You can't fix the problem if you don't know there's a problem or what it is.

8. **Treatment outcomes:** This metric measures the success in improving patients' sleep-related breathing disorders. Tracking treatment outcomes can help evaluate the effectiveness of different treatment approaches and guide decision-making for future treatment plans.

9. **Overhead and expenses:** What does it cost to run the practice? Evaluate your overhead expenses, including salaries, rent, utilities, lab fees, subscriptions, disposables, and other operating expenses. Monitoring this can help you identify opportunities for cost-savings, which directly affect your bottom line. Do you have unnecessary software subscriptions? Can you negotiate more

favorable lab fees? Are bulk discounts available for your HST supplies?

10. **Insurance reimbursement:** Which payors reimburse handsomely, and which ones pay a relative pittance? Should you go in-network with some payors? Are you a Medicare provider? How does this impact your reimbursement? Maximizing insurance reimbursement is crucial for maintaining financial stability and profitability in your sleep practice. Work closely with your biller.

11. **Marketing metrics:** Communicate consistently with your marketing partner. You need to know what's working and what isn't. What's the return on investment (ROI) on that activity? Let's say you're buying ads on social media. How many impressions, click-throughs, and calls are you getting from these efforts? How many new patient calls did you get? How many scheduled an appointment? Most important, how many agreed to proceed with treatment? If your phone is ringing off the hook, but patients aren't scheduling, that's a problem. If you don't assess these stats, you can't determine next steps. You shouldn't understand the minutiae related to buying Google Adwords or Facebook ads—that's what your marketing partner is for—but there's no excuse for not paying attention to your numbers. If you don't understand the metrics, pull a Denzel Washington from *Philadelphia,* and tell them to explain it to you like you're a four-year-old.

You wouldn't give someone a sleep test and then ignore the results, nor would you deliver a device without follow-up. Your accountant wouldn't just email you an annual P&L report without any commentary. Gathering this data is half the battle. Reviewing it at regular intervals and making appropriate adaptations is the other half. Weekly or monthly meetings with your sleep team are recommended so you can discuss where you're at and what needs to change.

W.O.W. JAGDEEP BIJWADIA

Author's note: Dr. Jagdeep Bijwadia is the sleep medicine collaborative archetype. He is board-certified in Internal Medicine, Pulmonary Medicine, and Sleep Medicine. Dr. Bijwadia serves as the medical director for several organizations and has lectured extensively on the topic of medico-dental collaboration in sleep. I don't know about the ramifications associated with human cloning, but if we could clone Dr. Bijwdia, the rewards would probably be worth the risk. —Jason Tierney

Dentists in my experience live in a world where results are exact and reproducible. A fraction of a millimeter separates the success or failure of a good crown fitting. Teeth are perfectly aligned with orthodontics. implants allow predictable, measurable, and exact results. Your procedure is either a success or not. Black and white.

In contrast, sleep medicine is all shades of gray. We measure the severity of apnea using the AHI, but definitions of AHI differ based on how much oxygen desaturation is required to define an event. Different sleep devices often give disparate results. The physiology of sleep apnea varies by sleep stage, sleep position, medications, and alcohol, to give just a few examples. There is variability in AHI from night to night. Your "baseline disease" is not so well defined.

Once treatment starts, the standard definition of success rests on improving the AHI. After you optimize treatment with an oral appliance, you retest to see if the AHI has normalized. Given the variability of the baseline AHI, you often come across patients whose AHI has improved but not normalized.

My message is that it is OK! Not every treatment works, not every measure is exact, and more than one treatment may be needed. Also, not every sleep symptom is related to sleep apnea. You have not failed if you are unable to bring the AHI to less than 5. Sometimes a 50 or 60 percent improvement from baseline is the best you can achieve, and in some patients (for example someone who starts with an AHI of 100 and has repeatedly failed CPAP), that is an excellent outcome. Do not strive for the "fraction of a millimeter standard of success." No physician expects that. Get comfortable with gray.

EMPLOYEE REVIEWS ARE YOUR FRIEND

As you walk into your office, the tension is palpable. Everyone's on edge.

"We've gotta talk," your sleep assistant declares, matter of factly.

"OK, I just got here, what's up?"

Like a waiting rattler, she uncoils, "I've been here for two years, and I haven't had a raise. I got an offer from Dr. Meter's office, and I don't want to quit, but I guess I'm gonna have to."

"I see. Um, uh, OK. I don't know what to say. When do you plan to leave?" Still holding your lunch and your laptop, you ask, "Can we talk about this later?" Ambushed. How did it happen? What could you have done differently? What is their problem?

Employee reviews may be one of the least electrifying, but also one of the most important facets of operating a successful dental sleep practice. Most practices overlook reviews altogether. The rest have an unstructured process that is only used when a team member asks for a raise. That's a bummer. If you don't have a formal review process, many team members will perform below expectations and will soon stagnate. In *The Hard Thing About Hard Things,* Ben Horowitz writes, "In a vacuum of feedback, there is almost no chance that your company will perform optimally … directions without corrections will seem fuzzy and obtuse."

A codified review process clearly defines employee goals, memorializes accountability, and engages team members in the process of mapping their futures. This motivates them to contribute to the practice's growth. Some HR consultants offer review templates and guidance on review processes.

It's been an iterative process, but I've found the steps described here to be instrumental in professional development.

Employee review trends come and go. Some involve scoring employees on criteria such as punctuality and dress code conformity. These criteria don't increase productivity, decrease waste, or improve patient satisfaction. Showing up on time? Wearing the proper uniform? You're not managing second graders; you're operating a premier dental sleep medicine practice.

Then there are 360-degree reviews that solicit anonymous input from co-workers. At first glance, this may seem like a good idea. It eliminates blind spots by getting information from colleagues who work with the employee in various capacities. Unfortunately, it also allows them to settle old scores, and it can compel people to add their two cents even when they have little of substance to contribute. I've received useful, actionable feedback in these reviews. I've also seen comments such as the following, submitted behind a cloak of anonymity:

"I don't work closely with Jason, so I don't know why I'm filling this out, but I really like his suits and ties."

"Jason works too much and expects other people to do the same."

"I don't like Jason's suits and ties."

Reviews provide opportunities to emphasize behaviors you want to see more of and those you want to discourage. They define specific goals to be met. Reviews also give team members uninterrupted time with you to candidly open up about aspirations, concerns, and salary issues. Finally, it's an opportunity for you to discuss the practice's strategy and concrete ways that team members can execute on it.

Together, you acknowledge the team member's wins, collaborate on ways to improve their shortcomings, and state ways in which they can develop while contributing to achieving the practice's goals. In a previous section, you read about the importance of providing real-time feedback. Because you're doing that, the review process should really be a formality. A proper review is devoid of surprises.

Described below is a utilitarian process that doesn't take a lot of time, and the payoffs are like hitting the jackpot. You move toward greater harmony in your practice, and your team actively contributes to suggesting new pathways for personal, professional, and practice growth. They know what you want, and you know where they are and where they want to go.

HOW IT WORKS

Consider delivering the first review at 90 days and subsequent reviews yearly thereafter. The former lets you evaluate initial performance and set goals while the latter gives you opportunities to assess performance over the longer term, ensuring that their goals and performance are still aligned with those of the practice.

Two weeks before the scheduled review date, send the team member a copy of your practice's self-assessment form. You can see an excellent example of a self-assessment form later in this section. Instruct them to thoughtfully complete the document and return it to you no later than one week before the review. Upon receiving their self-assessment, take a blank review form, fill it in, and then compare it to their self-assessment form. Identify trends and areas you want to focus on. Then revise the document with this information and specific examples to bolster key points.

Your aim is to memorialize the employee's past performance, along with their future goals. When an employee isn't meeting expectations, you can reference the document and identify which behaviors do not meet your stated goals. This empowers you to coach their performance or take disciplinary measures without hesitation. You can track their progress, and then, when review season rolls around, you can gleefully dole out salary increases.

Avoid the "recency effect" and cite specific supporting examples from the entire review period, not just the past few weeks. Don't review personalities; rather, focus on behaviors and tie them to outcomes. For example, don't say:

"It seems like you don't take the work seriously or you just don't care."

Consider this instead:

"In March, you were more than 20 minutes late on four occasions. This set the schedule behind, and two patients were forced to reschedule, which lost money for the practice."

This also applies to favorable feedback. For example, don't say:

"You're a team player and everyone loves you."

Instead, try this:

"Your willingness to step in to fill the sleep champ role has been great for the practice. The new screening protocol you created is leading to more new sleep patients each month. Several patients have told me that your communication style is what made them really want to get treated."

Next, consider the employee's goals and capabilities, and the goals of the practice. Use this information to document S.M.A.R.T. goals for the coming period. Finalize a clean version of the review, taking all of this information into account. Employee reviews often contain vague goals that don't grow the practice or the team member. I'm talking about things like "work smarter, not harder to grow referrals," and "focus on showing up on time on the days you have your kids." Goals like this mandate the minimum (and might be illegal) and hitting the target is usually met with a pithy cost-of-living increase. This can lead to resentment from dentists who feel, justifiably, that they're rewarding mediocrity. At the same time, team members can get peeved. They're unchallenged, untapped, and underpaid.

They want more out of you. You want more out of them. Sensible goals are a win-win.

SELF-ASSESSMENT AND REVIEW FORM

PREVIOUS GOALS

Goal	Actions	Deadline	Progress Notes

What steps has the team member taken since their last review to develop professionally?

What steps has the team member taken since their last review to positively impact our practice and the patients we serve?

What specific strengths does the team member possess and how have they utilized them for the benefit of our team, practice, and our patients? How can the team member further cultivate and leverage these strengths in the future? Be specific with the details and deadlines.

What are the team member's specific areas for improvement? How have they manifested, and what impact has it had on our stakeholders (team, patients, practice)? What specific steps will be taken to improve in the future? Be specific with details and deadlines.

NEW GOALS

Goal	Actions	Deadline	Progress Notes

Team Member Signature   Date

_____   _____

Review goals should clearly tie assigned activities to outcomes. For example, if the goal is an additional 20 physician referrals each month, assign your marketing rep to visit five new physicians' offices every week.

If you want to streamline appointment documentation and billing processes with a new EMR, ask your sleep champion to gather information, compare options, and coordinate with the software vendor and your team to implement the solution. Now, let's get down to brass tacks.

Near the end of the day before the review, tell the team member that you're providing them with copies of their review and self-assessment. Encourage them to review the documents so you can have a productive discussion. Advise them to look for trends and areas in which they strongly agree or disagree.

Begin the review at the appointed time. Don't reschedule and don't start late. Doing so infers the review is unimportant. Acknowledge that it's an unconventional review method. "Thanks for taking the time to thoughtfully complete your self-assessment. This hour is yours, and we can talk about whatever you want, but I do want to spend some time discussing any trends you've identified, points you strongly agree or disagree with, and your goals so we're in alignment going forward. How does that sound?"

"Sounds good," the team member replies.

"Cool, so to kick things off, what trends or recurring themes stood out to you in the review?"

After talking about trends, areas of excellence, and opportunities for improvement, segue to reviewing the upcoming period's goals. I recommend reading the goals verbatim to ensure absolute clarity. Gain agreement, inform them of any salary changes, and have them sign a copy of the review form. Keep the signed copy for your records.

All this may sound labor-intensive, but it isn't. It does require a bit of effort from you, your office manager, sleep champion, and whoever else is involved in the review process. However, it saves enormous time and energy in the long run by creating alignment, clarifying expectations, and accelerating progress.

A PENNY FOR MY THOUGHTS

"Impatience with actions, patience with results." —Naval Ravikant

A couple paragraphs ago I mentioned salary changes. How much should you pay a sleep champion? What about a sleep assistant or marketer? That swings wildly based on your market and other variables. I can tell you with certitude that if your team's salaries are closely connected to the value they create, they will behave more like "owners" who are invested in the success of the practice. They'll take more initiative and think more innovatively.

However, do not overpay an employee because they threaten to take their instruments elsewhere. If you give in to their demands, you're just rewarding an incompetent employee. This sets an undesirable cascade of events into motion. There's a negative impact on your profitability, creating an inflated salary benchmark for everyone on your team. The employee isn't any more capable, but your resentment level is ramped up. Other team members will feel it. If the individual is leaving so they can make significantly more money somewhere else, then you are likely underpaying them, but if they want to leave over a few bucks a month, they're not part of your vision.

Bite the bullet, let them leave, and learn from the experience. Use the lessons you learn from this book to find the right fit. Hire slowly. Pay slightly higher than market value. Recounting Yasiin Bey's views on employee compensation, Talib Kweli, writes, "You know how to thank people? You pay them." Treat team members well, follow the principles you've read thus far, and create opportunities for bonuses or profit-sharing.

Check it out: establishing meaningful metrics to track performance should be a cardinal concern. Your team's review goals should move your practice toward improved metrics. Be careful not to substitute productivity metrics for optimal patient care. Evaluate what's working and what isn't. Don't cut corners or trade short-term gain for long-term pain. Don't do an FMR on a sleep patient that was referred to you by another dentist. Keep referring back to physicians who refer to you, and remember that not every outcome is quantifiable. Be the best clinician, leader, and human you can possibly be. That's your most important goal. Data matters, but what you do with it matters more. Let's pivot.

W.O.W. SCOTT CRAIG

Author's note: Scott Craig is the CEO of Midwest Dental Sleep Center, which has multiple locations throughout the Chicago area. He's contributed to oft-cited DSM research, written numerous articles, and lectured to many industry groups. Scott is an erudite dude who grasps the clinical and business aspects of DSM best practices equally. —Jason Tierney

The way to success in the sleep field is listening to our customers; by customers, I'm talking about patients and referring physicians. The mission is to identify their pain points and obstacles to progress and figure out how to overcome them. How do we do that? We listen.

Years ago, we wanted to scale our business across multiple locations, which required a systematic approach to care that would keep us accountable. To do that, we needed to map and measure the patient experience, while also tracking patient outcomes. Every practice should have tools to measure feedback during the patient journey. We take this very seriously.

Eventually we identified three key areas where we can infuse value for our customers:

1. Cost – This can be affected by type of insurance; whether we're in or out-of-network with a payor; overhead such as lab, facility, and staffing costs; and payor allowed amounts. This list isn't exhaustive, but it provides a peek at several of the factors we study that may impact cost.

2. Access to care – We consider the geographic location of the practice; the referring physicians' familiarity with OAT; treatment side-effects; severity of disease; and chair time. All of these are way stations along the patient journey that must be evaluated. Where can we remove pressure that blocks access to care?

3. Quality – This covers just about everything under the sun. What's the culture of the practice? How much emphasis is placed on customer service and communication? From the practice management system and the EHR being utilized to the documentation, coding, and reimbursement processes—how can we add more value? We look at the equipment that's being used, such as digital scanners and the CAD-CAM appliances themselves. We learn about our referral sources and how they communicate with patients, how they position oral appliance therapy. Do we need to coach them? Does our team have the necessary education? What additional training do they need? What is our treatment efficacy? What do we need to do differently?

These are all points we look at to improve cost, access to care, and the quality of the experience. We want to provide the maximum number of patients with the highest quality care at the lowest cost.

Getting deeper into the weeds, we dove into all the patient journey touchpoints, starting at the point of referral to patient intake to impressions, delivery appointment, one-month follow-up, the efficacy study, and ongoing follow-up. If we provide value at every one of these steps, we can disrupt a broken system to improve care and build something better.

I spend a lot of time looking at financial reports, examining the data, applying the scientific method, and teasing out stories that we can use to build value at each step. We use this information to build custom reports that automate insight.

Here's a real-life example: A referral source sends three new patient referrals. Our intake coordinators note that the faxed referrals were received. This triggers the process to call the patients and schedule visits. We look at the day-sales-outstanding (DSO) report to see if the patients were scheduled. How long did it take? If they decided not to schedule, why didn't they? What happened? Are we too far away? Are we out of network? Is there any consistent pattern with patients not appointing when referred from that office? Did our team's script cause the patient to decline?

Oftentimes, patterns emerge. We might see that all three patients have Cigna insurance and a high out-of-pocket cost. This might prompt us to consider going in-network with the payor. Or maybe the patients all have low or no out-of-pocket costs. This could tell us something different. We might investigate further and find that patients referred from this provider convert at a lower rate than those referred by other providers. We could uncover that Dr. Smith communicates with her patients about OAT in a very different way than other MDs do. This provides us with an opportunity to go meet with Dr. Smith, provide more education, and improve the relationship.

In the above examples, I mentioned the DSO report. This report, along with efficacy reports, are the primary sources of truth in our practice. Here's a little bit about how we use them:

- *DSO reporting* gives us the soup to nuts accounting of the referral source, insurance carrier, and comprehensive patient demographic information. It's a time-based report that tracks the amount of time from when a patient was referred to us until a claim was submitted for therapy.

  Our goal is to use this information to minimize that window of time and maximize the number of people going through it. What factors along the way increase the time? The report is our objective safety net to prevent patients from falling through the cracks.

  Maybe the problem is that the referral source is chronically not providing us with the necessary documentation to get the patient moving. Perhaps the patient came in but didn't move forward with impressions. Why? Is it possibly because they had other dental issues?

The DSO report will continue to age, so we need to continue working with that patient to clean the report up. We work to ensure that our team executes a follow-up protocol to be certain that we're communicating with that patient and the referral source.

- *Efficacy reports* also help determine our direction. If a patient's treatment wasn't efficacious, why not, and where do we go from there? In DSM, we spend a lot of time worrying about oral appliances, but I spend more energy focusing on how we're going to get patients treated when OAT fails. If we focus only on OAT, we're no better than the one-size-fits-some-sometimes modalities that failed.

  The sleep field is fundamentally flawed. There's endless discussion about how we haven't identified the millions of patients that might benefit from treatment. The equally concerning issue is the astronomical number of people who've been treated unsuccessfully and then basically ignored. We're open-minded about treatment options. Dental sleep practices should serve as the quarterback for all dental solutions for OSA and snoring. We need to provide the continuity of care throughout the journey.

With enough passion and drive, any practice can overcome these barriers and do what we've done. Create a culture in your practice that makes everyone responsible for this. I was taught at an early age that our reputation is all we have in life. We take a lot of pride in creating something we believe in. The patient is the purpose at every level. This business is my life's work. It's a reflection of me, my sister, and my father, of who we are and what we do.

You need to have great backend systems to standardize and automate as much as possible. This helps you pull meaningful data, which tells a story. With this, you can make appropriate pivots. When explaining why we make changes, we always tie it to the patient's best interest. When you communicate from that perspective, it puts the focus on how you as a team can improve the patient's experience.

We do very basic things. We do the work. The numbers matter, but only because they represent the people. We use data to navigate the ship, and the direction is always tied to the patient's best interests. Always. That's why we succeed, and if you're reading this, you can too. There's hard work, uncertainty, and pain. But that's true of anything good. It's worth it.

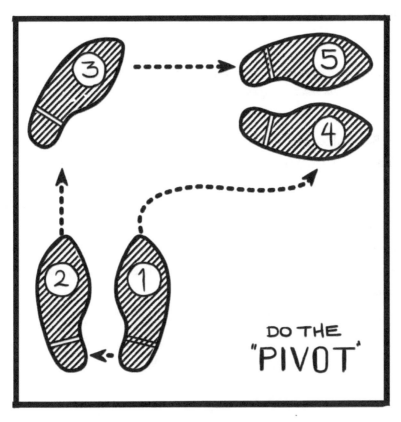

DO THE
"PIVOT"

FIG. 18 "PIVOT"

PIVOT *VERB*

1: to adapt or improve by adjusting or modifying something (such as a product, service, or strategy)

"The definition of insanity is doing the same thing over and over and expecting different results." —quote commonly misattributed to Albert Einstein

Dr. Ben Bedder treated 20–30 sleep patients every month for three years. Both of his referral sources sold their practices, and, abruptly, everything stopped. Now he treats zero sleep patients per month. He hasn't hired a physician marketing rep or set up lunch-and-learns with other potential referral sources, nor has he partnered with a marketing firm to promote his practice. So, what does he do? He just keeps attending courses and calling sales reps to ask what he should do. Now, five years later, nothing has changed for him.

Talking about what used to work isn't going to resurrect those glory days. Medicare guidelines will change. Remember Same or Similar? Did you capitalize on the unfortunate PAP recall? Were you able to pivot fast enough? Philips certainly failed on that front.

Payors will curveball the required documentation without notice. Labs change materials. Your sleep assistant might quit and move out of state. And your best referral sources sell their practices. Maintaining the status quo and hoping things change will not lead to improvement.

Remember when plans to "Netflix and chill," required at least ten days advance notice? Netflix started out as a DVD rental service. Its extensive selection of videos was a competitive advantage over brick-and-mortar rental spots. You'd visit Netflix's site and select a DVD, and they'd mail it to your house. Eventually they pivoted to a flat-rate subscription-based model and you could order multiple movies at a time and keep them for extended periods sans the specter of incurring the dreaded late fees. Slipping the DVD out of the red sleeve, you scrupulously examined the disc for scratches, with the same trepidation you feel when a top referral source comes in for their first appliance follow-up appointment. Imagine waiting ten days only to find out that *Weekend at Bernie's 2* was scratched and unplayable beyond the opening credits.

Streaming technology was a seismic disruptor for the DVD rental business. Reed Hastings and his Netflix team were attuned to shifts in customer preferences and realized the need to pivot again to capitalize on the trend. Buh-bye Blockbuster—hello, Netflix and the new age of streaming. Another Netflix pivot followed as they segued from DVD rentals to streaming subscriptions. Massive overhauls were required. Nearly everything had to change: the financial model, the delivery method, and the employees needed to run the business. They provided severance checks and employment agency services to the employees who once stuffed envelopes with DVDs. Now they needed data analysts, behavioral psychologists, and top-tier programmers.

The pivots roll on as Netflix endlessly curates their colossal library of content, while also emerging as award-winning content creators. Through the company's evolution, it has continually evaluated market shifts, changing customer tastes, technological advancements, competitive pressures, and global economic changes. Not every pivot was monumental—the next video in a series plays automatically now, and trending videos are displayed—but each pivot moves the business to new heights, cementing its position as a global home-entertainment leader.

This continuous improvement is a prime example of *kaizen*, a Japanese term translated loosely as "change for good." Like the five whys discussed earlier, the kaizen concept was popularized inside of the Toyota Motor Company. The emphasis on continuous improvement permeates every level of the organization, from strategic planning and sales to every aspect of the manufacturing line. Each individual and every function is empowered with the autonomy to evaluate processes and identify ways to eliminate waste and improve productivity.

In most instances, changes aren't historic earth-shatterers; they're incremental. In a sleep practice, examples might include things like:

- Changing case presentation verbiage to overcome common objections, leading to higher case acceptance.

- Updating the sleep consultation room's décor to make it more inviting.

- Having HST units available so patients can leave their appointments with tests.

- Using a service that provides patients with a link to leave online reviews.

- Revising the script for the front desk when answering sleep questions so more patients schedule during the initial call.

- Ramping up your sleep physician outreach to offset the PAP recall's shortage so patients still get the therapy they need.

Nothing changes if nothing changes. Avoid succumbing to the sunk cost fallacy. Don't be afraid to terminate a team member just because they've worked for you for a few calendars. If you bought several testing units, but then realize that there's a service that gets more of your patients tested with less burden and expense for you and your team, use the service. Don't moor yourself to those units just because you already bought them.

Dr. Ben Bedder devoted serious time and effort to developing those once fruitful referral relationships. Now they're gone, and yet he keeps hoping things will somehow go back to normal. In this case, hope is the enemy. It deprives him of agency. No outside entity is coming to save his practice. It didn't have to end this way for Dr. Bedder, though. Failure wasn't inevitable. It could have served as an inflection point. Because you've instituted the best practices from the previous sections, your team has the latitude to evaluate processes and pivot as needed. Baby steps toward continuous improvement multiplied by time equals big results. You'll fare better than Bedder.

After treating sleep patients for a while, some practices reach a plateau. Case volume might flatten. Referrals might start to dip. Even the best laid plans sometimes go astray. This isn't the end of the road. It's merely an indicator that it's time to pivot. You can redirect your efforts and energy.

Progress isn't always linear. Sometimes we take three steps forward and one back. Paraphrasing C. S. Lewis, to get nearer to your goals, don't move forward blindly. If you took a wrong turn somewhere, continuing on that path will just get you more lost. Turn around and get back on the right one. Course correct and get back on track. Pivot.

W.O.W. STEVE CARSTENSEN

Author's note: As co-owner of Premier Sleep Associates, an exclusive sleep practice in Bellevue, Washington, I don't know how Dr. Steve Carstensen finds the time to grace more daises than just about any other DSM educator while also serving as the Editor-in-Chief of Dental Sleep Practice magazine. It doesn't end there: he's also an audiophile and co-author of The Clinician's Handbook for Dental Sleep Medicine.
—Jason Tierney

It's tough to face up to your mistakes. In the heady days of dreaming about Premier Sleep's amazing future impact on community health, Carrie and I had only expansive thoughts. We knew signing up for a bigger, newer space was risky, but surely the trajectory of referrals and people seeking better breathing would support the overhead.

6 years in, not so much - creativity flowed. What if we had other providers use our space part-time? How about seeing patients in other offices, in addition to our own, to add income? Do we add services to increase patient and cash flow? Is the answer, through attrition and less pleasant means, to reduce employee investment?

Lots of thinking, talking, meeting time, brainstorming ideas. We invested hundreds of hours in an exciting plan to merge Premier Sleep with a medical-dental clinic that fell through three weeks before our lease was signed over.

Lease signed over? Indeed! When one is open to possibilities, good things arrive. The medical clinic next door came calling one day, seeking room for expansion. Problem solved – they bought our lease and most of our equipment, freeing us from the overhead.

We didn't want to shut Premier Sleep down (it was discussed) so we pushed the merger idea – putting a lot of our eggs into that basket. When the lawyers shut it down, Carrie and I had to figure it out or be homeless. We found a small dental office that needed only cleaning and some fresh paint for our vision to continue.

Healthcare clinics are more than about location, though. We had to change our workflow, our presentation, our connection with our patients. Our front desk person moved out of state, becoming a voice on the phone instead of the friendly greeter. More scrambling. The new little spot had no room for our beloved cone beam machine, so it was sold to our favorite orthodontist. Only one room has a door for private medical conversations. One desk for two doctors to share.

What makes this work? Our partnership – there could be no better. We take things in stride, stay curious about possibilities, and diligently examine choices. Once decisions are made, energy flows and progress happens. A universal abundance philosophy reigns. Hard work is required, for sure, but the belief in each other buoys each of us over the rough patches without ever feeling more than transient dispiritedness. Our team feels the drive to creativity and the safety to take chances to improve, with an abundance mentality.

SHOULD YOU MARKET SLEEP?

"The riches are in the niches, but the fortune is in the follow-up." —*Pat Flynn*

Picture a Venn diagram with three circles, labeled "Dentist," "Physician," and "Public." The overlapping intersection is "lack of awareness." Most patients are unaware of the impacts of poor sleep on their overall health, and even if they some inkling, they probably don't know about OAT as a potential treatment option. Contrary to many dentists' false assumptions, most physicians don't have much sleep education, and those who do usually have very little knowledge as to the role dentists can play.

Then there are dentists. The fact that I've coined it "The 100 Club" and not "The 100,000 Club" is evidence of dentistry's lack of awareness. Most dentists aren't attuned to sleep issues. They don't know how to identify patients, which precision medical devices to use, how to collaborate with physicians—all the things this book is about. Dental sleep medicine doesn't have a CPAP problem or an insurance problem; it has an awareness problem, and marketing can play a key role in raising awareness.

Do you ever get bored and actually look at those discount coupon envelopes you receive from direct mail companies? Among the coupons for cheap dry cleaning and backyard awning installation, you'll find a handful for dental practices. They typically feature one of the following: a 20-year-old poorly doctored headshot of the dentist, an unflattering group photo of the dentist surrounded by the team, or stock images of smiling people. The aesthetics of these ads are indiscernible from the ads for retirement planning or chiropractic services.

The similarities don't end with the images. The cookie-cutter approach extends to the ad copy and promotional offers, too. Did you know that every dental practice that mails to me is "now accepting new patients?" Did you know they offer "free X-rays and exams for new patients?" Guess what? They also do same day crowns and whitening.

Every. Single. Effing. One of them.

They look alike *and* they sound alike. This results in dental practices futilely fighting in the over-saturated red ocean in a plunge to the commoditized bottom. So, as a *sui generis* practice, what do you do? What's your competitive advantage? Why should they make an appointment with you? I'll give you a hint: Don't do what they're doing. Pivot by promoting snoring and sleep apnea treatments. That'll make you stand out.

The restaurant industry is a tough business, and most establishments fail within the first five years. In the throes of the COVID pandemic, my friends Brian and Bradley opened a small restaurant in an area of St. Louis that was already teeming with restaurants. *Even smart people can make dumb decisions*, I thought. And then I heard about the concept: "Terror Tacos," a horror movie-themed vegan taco restaurant that only plays death metal music. Hearing this, I clamored to call Brian and urge him to nix the crazy idea.

Then, I checked it out. The food was amazing. Sitting in the restaurant noshing on their delectable tacos, I watched my fellow diners relish their experience. Older vegans loved the food and novel experience while the younger crowd dug the vibe and the unique cocktails as much as the "Carnage Asada" burritos replete with house-made seitan. They market their restaurant via social media, email newsletters, community events, and word-of-mouth. I've eaten there at least ten times, and I tell anyone who will listen about how great it is. After three years of honing processes and scaling operations, Terror Tacos is eyeing expansion into new markets.

Don't overlook opportunities to stand out and stand apart. It doesn't get much more banal than email out-of-office responders. "Hi, I'm out of the office until June 3rd. If you need immediate assistance, please call …" A friend's version of this features all the salient details about who to call in her absence but also adds flair. "I'll return on June 3rd, assuming I'm not eaten by an alligator or quit working to become a semi-professional Scrabble player." People love these emails so much they forward them to their friends, and they've become points of conversation.

At a sleep conference with umpteen vendors vying for dentists' attention, we were given one minute to introduce ourselves from the lectern. One presentation droned into the next: "Hi, I'm Jimmy Clone and I work for Clone Lab. We make the same products as everyone else." I took the mic and introduced myself, shared our company's tight elevator pitch, and told everyone that I won on *Wheel of Fortune* but failed to solve the final puzzle. I invited everyone to our Booth 456 to find out what the puzzle was. Same 60 second opportunity, but guess whose booth was swarmed by prospective dentist clients?

It works for restaurants, authors, and dental practices. Look different. Sound different. Set yourself apart and set sail for the limitless blue ocean, beyond competition and on to the horizon. Promote CPAP alternatives. Highlight the free consultation and possibility of an improved version of themselves. Use images of healthy middle-aged couples living their best lives: riding bikes together, walking on the beach, smiling in bed. Below are a couple of copy concepts for your consideration.

"Sick of Snoring? Tired of Sleeping Alone? Singing the CPAP Blues? Contact Dr. Diva for a Free Consultation Today."

"Is Snoring Keeping You Up at Night? Schedule a Free Consultation Today So You Can Sleep Better Tonight."

I can hear you now. "Yeah, Jason, but it's 2023. I never look at junk mail. Everyone finds their dentist online."

That's partially true. It is 2023, and you probably rarely look at your "junk" mail. Interestingly, Murphy Research recently conducted a survey of 3250 U.S. consumers and found that 88 percent of "key purchase decisions" across retail and financial categories are discussed at home. Which means that a uniquely targeted message could really keep your DSM practice top-of-mind among your target demographics. According to a report from InfoTrends, 65 percent of millennials made a purchase as a result of direct mail, and 82 percent of the coveted baby boomer population reported being more likely to buy from a business that mails them.

Like your stock portfolio, marketing is a bit of a gamble, and, like a proper portfolio, diversity is key. You shouldn't put all your eggs in the direct mail basket. Talk to prospective patients where they are via the media they use. A well-managed, properly executed digital marketing campaign for your sleep practice can generate desirable returns.

You're a smart cookie, but you should absolutely outsource your online marketing. It's a very specialized, ever-changing niche. Don't trust the job to your 22-year-old nephew because "he's always posting on TikTok and playing video games." What does he know about the lifetime value of a customer, conversion paths, TOFU, MOFU, BOFU, and CTR?

Google Ads and other social media ad campaigns can be hyper-focused. This means you can target specific age demographics, professions, and geographic areas. These pay-per-click (PPC) marketing channels also allow you to allocate a reasonable, flexible budget and track performance in real time.

Some practices have even used "geofencing," a marketing tactic that targets anyone entering a specific geographic area. They might send ads to the phones of people visiting a nearby sleep lab or DME provider. Little too intrusive? Maybe it is. I'm not recommending this tactic; I'm just letting you know about some of the low and high-tech options out there. Launch a strong PPC campaign, enhanced by focused social media marketing and complemented by low cost/high yield direct-mail promotion, and you'll have the most fruitful channels covered.

As with offline direct mail marketing, be sure your digital campaigns have a focused message that cuts through the clutter. Many people don't like their CPAPs. Most people are embarrassed by their snoring or annoyed as hell with their bed partner's snoring. A lot of people desperately want better sleep and better health. Focus on this messaging. Incorporate compelling images that grab viewers' attention, and have a direct call-to-action. Give it time. Effective marketing usually requires multiple impressions. Whether it's Facebook ads, a poster in your waiting room, or a postcard in their mailboxes, each impression exposes them to your message.

Partner with a reputable, capable marketing company to promote your sleep practice. Leverage best practices while creating your unique message. It's not only OK to be different; it's a necessity. John Stuart Mill wrote, "That so few now dare to be eccentric marks the chief danger of the time."

WHAT'S UP, DOC?

In 2022, my bestest friend acquired an existing dental sleep practice. The previous owner paid a company six figures to give him the roadmap and resources to develop a DSM juggernaut. At its height, the practice treated 17 patients in one month.

Within three months of acquisition, my friend let go of most of the existing staff, hired new team members, and implemented their own processes and protocols that align closely with those enumerated in this book. They did something else, too, and this *x* factor made all the difference. Within six months, they were completing an average of 40 cases every month in that office.

My friend didn't pay anyone $100k to learn how to do this. They didn't even pay anything close to that for the practice. Guess what the game-changer was? Just guess.

Physician referrals.

Referrals didn't fall from the sky like manna from heaven. No one at the practice had magic referral dust. They made it happen, and so can you. The techniques aren't sexy, but they work. It isn't a proprietary process. It's not voodoo. The costs are nominal, and the payoff is bonkers. If you follow the recipe Angela shares in the W.O.W. section, you will realize more physician referrals. It's that simple. Are you ready to make it happen?

MORE PHYSICIAN MEETING JAZZ

"A young man comes up to me and he says, 'Mr. Shandling, can I talk to you for a second?' And I said, sure, what's up? He goes, 'You know I've only been in LA for a few months, and I want to do standup comedy. There's gotta be a secret, right? There's gotta be a shortcut.' I said, what are you talking about? He said,

'Well, you know, I hear about guys having to go work in clubs, and they have to do this, and they do this, and it's all about the work, and you gotta try jokes, and write jokes, but there's always a shortcut.

I said, No, there's no shortcut. There's literally no shortcut." —Garry Shandling

In the following pages, Angela masterfully downloads the tricks of the MD marketing trade for you. But first, here are a few more effective pointers shared by physician marketing gurus at other practices in The 100 Club:

- Forecast their potential concerns, questions, or misinformation. Don't be adversarial. Seize this opportunity to educate them so they can educate and refer their patients. Commonly heard objections from physicians include:

  I heard they don't work.

  They cost too much, so why can't they try one from Walgreens?

  Insurance doesn't cover them, and they have to pay cash.

  Someone complained that it caused side-effects like TMJ.

- Script your responses and internalize the info so you don't speak fluidly and fluently. Rehearse your script out loud. Trust me, this will help. It sounds drastically different coming out of your mouth than it looks on your MacBook screen. Acknowledge shortcomings up front, e.g., "OAT isn't always as effective as PAP at lowering AHI" or "We aren't in-network with some plans, but we do all we can to work with patients' coverage and minimize out-of-pocket expenses." This establishes credibility and builds trust, and, like glasses, research has shown that it makes you look smarter.

- Research the doctor and the practice by checking out their website and social media pages. Inquire about the practice from any shared contacts. Identify three or four noteworthy questions or conversation-sparking observations. Be prepared to talk less, ask questions, and listen. Request permission to discuss potential collaboration, and address ideas for a WIN-WIN relationship.

- Bring referral pads, treats, compelling research, and more. Some reps suggest bringing sample devices for grown-up show and tell. Have all the relevant materials ready to go.

After the meeting, the prospect might refer a patient before you get back to the office. Or multiple visits might be necessary. *Star Wars* and *Pulp Fiction* were both initially passed over by film executives, and multiple publishers passed on *Harry Potter,* which has sold more books than any other in history except *The Bible.* Don't be discouraged.

W.O.W. ANGELA KOWALESKI

Author's note: At the next annual sleep conference, try playing "Six Degrees of Angela Kowaleski." She's spent over two decades immersed in nearly every aspect of the sleep field and currently serves as Physician Liaison and COO for GoTo Sleep Center for CPAP Alternatives. Located throughout the Phoenix valley, GoTo's offices were built almost entirely on physician referrals. Angela knows her stuff, and if you turn her tips into action, you'll see results. —Jason Tierney

I've been blessed to learn from the best sleep educators and have literally worked every position in a sleep practice (except dentist, of course). I wear multiple hats, but I've spent most of the past five years focused on physician marketing. I used to encounter rooms of dentists who thought physicians didn't want to refer to them because of an aversion to oral appliance therapy. While only a minority of docs fit that description, sleep doesn't produce a strong signal for most MDs, and OAT barely registers as a blip.

My job is to change that, to raise awareness. I educate physicians and their teams about sleep. In some practices, I quash misinformation about dental sleep medicine, and then reeducate them so they understand that we're collaborators, not competitors. Then we alloy the education and camaraderie into new patients who will realize healthier, happier lives by seeking treatment at our practice.

Education is essential in marketing. Before you start knocking on doors and telling every Dr. Tom, Dr. Dick, and Dr. Mary to send all their mild, moderate, and PAP-noncompliant patients to you, I recommend doing some prep work. Know your product. Learn the science, abbreviations, acronyms, and everything in between. Commit to memory some statistics about OAT efficacy, PAP compliance rates, and other related info. Shore up any knowledge gaps by asking questions of colleagues and vendor partners, and doing some internet research.

Now that you know a thing or ten, it's time to get your marketing materials in order. Always leave something tangible at prospect offices that includes your branding. I use folders containing our name, business cards, referral forms, prescription pads, insurance list, and patient brochures. Depending on the office's experience and interest, I sometimes leave several relevant OAT case-study articles, too. *Here's a valuable pro tip*: Add a note at the bottom of your insurance list stating that you'll work with the patient to maximize their benefits even if you aren't currently participating with an insurance program.

It doesn't hurt to bring a small treat with you. Office personnel tend to engage more readily when they see a sweet reward for their time. This can help you circumvent the gatekeeper and get the office details you need. I usually spend around ten dollars on these treats at a discount club. Once you identify a prospect office as a new potential account, you can invest a little more with donuts or baked goods.

Keep your eyes peeled when you're commuting to a practice. You'll be astonished by how many other prospective offices you'll drive past. Because of this, keep double the supply of folders you think you need. You can always make an impromptu visit to one of these other offices.

Equipped with your sleep education and marketing materials, you might ask, what's next? Start with your local sleep centers and sleep physicians. Build rapport with them. They'll become the cornerstone of your sleep practice. Sleep centers prescribe CPAP, APAP, and other therapies, but times are changing, and the medical community's openness to OAT is greater than ever before. There is no one-size-fits-all treatment.

When researching local sleep centers, be sure to check whether the facility is an independent diagnostic testing facility (IDTF). IDTFs are diagnostic centers only and do not have prescribing doctors on staff. Develop a relationship with the IDTF, and ask them who their top referring offices or physicians are. This information can be worth its weight in gold. Pulmonary offices also present great opportunities. Pulmonologists boarded in sleep medicine get moved up the list. Next, look for neurology offices or ENT offices specializing in sleep.

After picking the low-hanging fruit—physicians specializing in sleep disorders—look for other specialty offices. One increasingly popular example is heart and arrhythmia. An estimated **40–50 percent of patients with atrial fibrillation have OSA,** and patients with sleep apnea have **four times the risk of developing A-fib.** Some internal medicine and primary care physicians now diagnose and treat sleep apnea, too.

This is spectacular news because it means more awareness and additional opportunities for collaboration. The concierge practice model is becoming more and more popular. In a nutshell, patients pay monthly or annual fees to see their physicians. These offices work to decrease the number of visits patients need. When approaching these offices, it's important to educate doctors and staff on the importance of treating sleep apnea due to its impact on overall health.

Don't forget the dental offices. Once my route is planned, I search nearby dental offices and pop in and leave our information. As you know, many dentists don't treat sleep. Now, they'll have your information to share with patients.

So many dentists think physicians intentionally ignore OSA and OAT. The truth is that it can almost always be traced to the lack of awareness. I can't count the number of times I've encountered well-educated, well-intentioned physicians with booming practices who just don't know much about sleep-disordered breathing. When I start making connections between sleep apnea and the health issues they see in their patients and advise how we may be able to help, the referrals almost always follow.

Details, details, and more details are key to mapping a perfect route. Calling offices in advance can help get the information needed to include or discount a new lead. Ask exploratory questions to learn more about the practice. Find out if they're treating OSA patients, prescribing oral appliance therapy, or ordering sleep tests. Ask permission to drop off some referral materials. The answer will almost always be "yes." Is there a specific referral coordinator to address the materials to? This information will allow you to walk into the office and ask for the person by name, once again helping you bypass that pesky gatekeeper. Since the pandemic began, more people answering phones for these offices are actually working remotely. Keep this in mind because they might not be current on everything going on at the office. If you believed initially that this office was a good one, then follow your gut.

Platforms such as Badger Maps, Sales Rabbit, and Salesforce are extremely helpful for optimizing your route, thereby saving you time and money. I just mentioned a few of the more popular options, and I've used Badger Maps for several years. I can input a specialty office such as "pulmonary," and then it populates the map with all the pulmonary offices in the vicinity. Google or other search engines can also be useful in creating a sales and marketing pipeline. Consider getting a free Rxvantage.com account, which lets you schedule lunches with practices via the site. Ultimately, how you use your CRM platform matters far more than which one you use. Every prospect visited or called should be documented in your system. Include every detail you can get.

Check out websites for alternative therapies, such as Inspire, exciteOSA, and Remede. Each site includes a tab to find physicians prescribing these therapies. The listed physicians are already treating sleep patients, making them great leads for you. What do they do with patients who don't qualify for treatment or were non-responsive to therapy? Retirement communities can also be great marketing spots. Facilities normally have a front office that can provide you with details about their newsletter, health events, and community health presentation opportunities.

Education? Check. Materials? Check. Route planned? Check. Let's go! Communicating effectively is key to developing consistent referral accounts that feed your practice. First impressions really do matter. A lot. Preparation is paramount, and personality goes along way. What sports memorabilia is in the office? What about their families? Details you ascertain from the visit and circle back to during later conversations will impress and build trust.

I cannot stress enough how important it is to remember the names of the people at the office. I promise you that when you go back to an office and call the front desk person by their name they'll be dazzled. Dale Carnegie was right: our own names are the sweetest sound. Get the front office person's name and introduce yourself and your practice, and give a sincere, but brief pitch about what you do. Know when the doctors are in or out of the office. Find out whether they're only providing telemedicine visits so you can provide a digital version of your brochure that they can send patients after visits. This may sound unimportant, but these small details can make a big difference. Be specific in your business and your mission.

Now you're getting somewhere. Routes have been completed and referrals are coming in. Documenting encounters and consistently tracking referrals are crucial to build momentum. Whether it's through a spreadsheet or your EHR, keep track of every referral. If patients don't proceed due to lack of insurance coverage or some other reason, always follow-up with them. CPAP patients should be called in 30 days to see if they're using their machine. Between the middle and end-of-year, circle back with patients who declined because of insurance issues. It's likely they've since met their deductibles. Think of this information as a rolling list of potential patients.

To lunch or not to lunch? That is the question. When setting up a lunch, be sure the office is truly interested in your business. If you ask an office if they prescribe oral appliances and they answer "yes," ask for more information. Do they refer out for an oral appliance once per year, or are they regularly sending their patients to another dentist all the way across town? How many patients are they sending each month? What does their ideal referral situation look like? Some reps like to do lunches on Fridays. The problem with that is that the weekend arrives, a new week begins, and you're last week's news. I prefer to do lunches earlier in the week, so staff and doctors see potential patients to refer while we're still top-of-mind.

Personal engagement and route tips. When you schedule a lunch, be sure to have a sign-in sheet. The one I use asks for name, position, and day and month of their birthday. I'm looking for the doctor or key staff member's birthday to surprise them with a sweet treat. Every sign-in sheet gets attached to the respective referral files and I add the birthdays on my marketing Google calendar.

After a lunch meeting, handwrite and mail a thank you card to key contacts. Follow up in person one week later to make another impression. For established, consistent referral accounts, visit them twice monthly.

Once you identify a key person in an office, try to obtain their personal cell phone number. I like to text my accounts randomly with a special cupcake delivery notice or pop-up pizza day. I try to do something relevant to the season or holiday, anything from Easter baskets to Halloween candy to donut day. I've created a holiday calendar with daily activities for office teams to participate in, follow our social media, and send me the daily challenge to be eligible for a special treat.

Follow-up is key. I've received referrals from offices on my first visit after they told me they didn't treat sleep patients. At the other end of the spectrum, I visited one office eight times before we received our first referral.

Don't be discouraged. Be confident. You have a purpose. You're not bothering the office; you're offering to help their patients while building your business.

The most important thing. Always ask for the business: ***"Which patients can I help you with TODAY?"***

MAKING THE LEAP TO A SLEEP-ONLY PRACTICE

"You can pay the price of winning and success or you can pay the price of losing and regret. The choice is yours." —Tim Grover

Almost every dentist bitten by the sleep bug has ambitions of shifting to a DSM-only practice. Most of us want our passion to be our career, especially if it means getting rewarded *more* for doing *less,* while also avoiding the type of drudgery that brings stress and premature gray hair.

Still, life doesn't stop. Bills have to be paid: kids' tuition, student loans, spouse's spending, ex-spouse's spending, volatile stock market, you know the drill. So, do you stay on the Sisyphean treadmill, but ratchet up your sleep marketing a couple notches, and at some point in the future shift to just sleep? Should you bring in an associate to see GP patients while devoting more of your time to sleep? Before Nike became the global behemoth we know today, Phil Knight sold shoes out of the trunk of his car while working as an accountant. In 1997, Larry Page tried to sell Google for a meager $2 million because he was concerned about the time it was taking from his PhD studies.

I've addressed rooms packed with dentists contemplating these same decisions. I understand your conundrum. I've been in a very similar situation. As an aspiring writer, I wanted to chuck everything, but, like you, I've gotta keep the lights on. I asked a couple of pals who've sold millions of books. One even landed a coveted spot on *Oprah.* One of these accomplished authors told me to keep working my "day job" and write at every available opportunity so my lifestyle isn't disrupted. The other advocated I jettison anything that interferes with writing.

With two conflicting recommendations, what'd I do? Well, of course I turned to my wife for the tie-breaker. She emphatically urged me to jump, to burn the ships and blaze forward.

Maybe you suffer from impostor syndrome. I certainly have. Who am I to write a book? Maybe you think an enviable sleep practice is something other people do, but not you. The truth is that we're all capable of making it happen. It just takes practice and time. The W.O.W. contributors in this book are living proof that it can be done.

What's right for you? Should you navigate the struggle of the juggle while focusing incrementally more and more on DSM? Should you sell the practice and vanquish the naysayers? Ultimately, it's up to you and your tie-breaker to decide, but Robert Quillen warns us against sitting on the fence: "Progress always involves risk. You can't steal second and keep one foot on first base."

W.O.W. STACEY LAYMAN

Author's note: The gratitude I feel to have Dr. Stacey Layman as my sleep dentist pales in comparison to the appreciation I have for her as a friend. She co-owns GoTo Sleep Center for CPAP Alternatives, which has several locations in the greater Phoenix area and consistently hovers around the top of The 100 Club. Her patients and team adore her. Dr. Layman also started a Facebook dental sleep medicine group with more than 5000 members. You've seen her on stages, on TV, and now in print. —Jason Tierney

When Jason asked me to write about how my business partner, Lesia and I built our sleep practice, it was the first time it hit me that our story is one that dentists really need to hear.

"CHEAPEST STARTUP EVER": That's our motto and our mantra. We say it to each other every time we consider a purchase or sign a new lease. Over many years of practice in both general dentistry and sleep, I've been approached by sales reps who always sing some version of the same song. It goes a little something like this, "Your ROI from buying my equipment will change your practice. Everyone is buying this or that. You *need* this; you *gotta have* that."

Here's the thing: When the recession of 2007 hit, I survived even as many others did not. They had beautiful offices filled with expensive chairs, cabinetry, and equipment. I can only imagine the levels of stress they must have been under. I never bought into the must-have mindset, but I was still a technologically advanced clinic.

When Lesia and I started our first stand-alone sleep office, we were keenly aware that it would take time to grow and become profitable. Our first office cost us less than $10k to launch. $10k! We didn't choose the best location with the nicest build-out; we leased a one-room space above the police rescue helicopter hangar.

Equipment-wise, we started with a front desk and one used chair purchased off Craigslist. It was old, but clean, and it worked perfectly. For our build-out, we bought two lower cabinets at IKEA, and Lesia's dad installed them for us. We brought in furniture from our own homes and set up a nice waiting room.

Eventually, we needed to add a second chair, and given that we were only renting a single room, we bought room dividers from a business supply website for a couple hundred bucks. The room didn't have sinks or X-ray equipment. It was very basic.

Bootstrapping our startup allowed us to reinvest in the company with a great staff, including an outside marketing rep, who built our referral network and became the concierge between the patient, the referring doctor, and our office. I suggest you go on as many lunch-and-learns with your rep, as often as you can. Get face-to-face time whenever possible with physicians.

Within a year, we grew to two locations. Two years later, we added a third. We're planning a fourth within the next 12 months, and it all started with one front office, one assistant, one doctor, a treatment/financial coordinator, and an outside rep. Lesia and I filled two of those roles and still do so today. We now have one front office, two assistants, a doctor, and a treatment coordinator for each office. We hire additional staff only when we can justify the cost. We're completely debt-free.

During COVID, we were able to continue paying our employees and ourselves. We had zero financial stress because we didn't owe anyone anything. Our technology over the years has grown slightly with digital intra-oral scanners and slightly higher-rent spaces in more desirable locations, but we're still always looking for the best deal. As the practice owner, you have responsibilities to your staff, your patients, and your family, to ensure success.

In my experience, the essential items you need to start a sleep practice include:

- A small space—less than 1200 sq ft—with a consult room and 1-3 exams rooms. Location is not important at first, but it does need to be in a safe area and be easy to find.

- The space doesn't need to be built out for medical or dental. Less is more. Sinks are a bonus but not a necessity.

- A digital intra-oral scanner as long as you can pay cash. Otherwise, take analog impressions.

- If the space is not built out the way you want it, paint it yourself and buy cabinets from Home Depot, IKEA, or somewhere comparable. Remember, you won't be in this space forever!

- Minimal supplies, such as BP cuff, stethoscope, hot and cold water kettle, Dixie cups, electric lab hand piece, AM Aligners, a couple of laptops, inexpensive DSM software, sample device models, a couple of regular desks depending on the space, a pen light, and a used dental, ENT or even gaming chair.

I'm sure I've missed some small items in this list, but you get the idea. Repeat our mantra—"cheapest startup ever"—every time you want to buy that new shiny thing. My last W.O.W. message to you is "just do it." Don't over think it. Follow the steps in this book, keep it cheap, and get it done.

THE BOOK OF
REVELATIONS

"And in the end, it's not the years in your life that count. It's the life in your years."
—*Abraham Lincoln*

Do ut des. It translates to, "I give so that you may give." People have asked me what my "why" is. The truth is, I stumbled into a career in sleep. For a long time, I found it interesting. There's so much to learn and countless business development opportunities in this nascent industry. However, sleep is not my passion. The reason I get up in the morning is (yeah, I know my circadian rhythm is the real reason I get up in the morning) to strive for improvement. Kaizen. I seek continual betterment for myself and those in my sphere of influence. I breathe to help others realize their potential. In helping them, I grow. Like the steps in this book, it's a cyclical process that will end when I stop breathing.

Too melodramatic? I don't mean to lay it on so thick, but this is literally life or death. For your patients, treatment may be the difference between a heart attack and lots more wiffle ball games with the grandkids; the difference between an overturned semi with multiple fatalities on the highway and a safe commute to the office. It could be the catalyst for change that may one day enable a daughter to become a mother, a grandmother, and the scientist who discovers a cure for cancer.

The healthcare landscape is changing. Practitioners who fail to adapt to new environments die. If you don't change, you, too, will go extinct. This is a do-or-die decision, not only for your patients, but also for your practice. Right now, the decision is yours. Later, it may not be. This book isn't a panacea for your practice. There's no magic elixir. However, the concepts you just read can help you not only survive, but thrive in this new world.

It won't always be smooth sailing, but it will be worth it, and you can do it. Albert Camus wrote, "In the depths of winter, I finally learned that within me there lay an invincible summer." You are resilient. The average life span today means you'll have around 80 Thanksgiving dinners with your family. How many do you have left? This revelation might leave you feeling a bit nihilistic. It shouldn't. Stop doing things you don't want to do, and focus your energies on things that matter. Instead of asking, "What's the point," ask "Where's the meaning?" Ask yourself these questions. Why am I doing this and where is the meaning? If the answers are unsatisfactory, change what you're doing. This isn't a one-and-done exercise. Like all the principles in this book, they should be practiced for the rest of your life.

Sometimes it will be easy. Other times it will be strenuous. Real change requires the initial investment of energy to kick things off. Chemistry teaches us that activation energy is delivered to start a reaction, destroying the current state, and transforming it into something new. New connections form, and it is impossible to return to the previous state. It doesn't end there. If we opt not to allocate sufficient activation energy, we will fail to achieve the desired results. After repeated attempts, we become jaded and think it's mission impossible. That's why so many drunks fail to stay sober, coups fail to turn into effective new governments, and dentists give up on DSM.

The push must be sufficient to muscle the reaction through to its conclusion. If we want a productive garden, we can't just till the soil and scatter a few seeds. To reap an abundant harvest, we must engage in the process and commit fully to it. Epictetus asks us, "If you didn't learn these things in order to demonstrate them in practice, what did you learn them for?"

Inertia is our nemesis. If we rest on our laurels, tallying wins becomes harder. Think back to the last time you went on vacation and took a pause on your diet and exercise regimen. Getting back on the wagon was a challenge. During the development of this book, I sporadically took time off from writing. Every day away equated to a week of re-acclimation. Don't let this happen with your sleep practice. Pedal to the metal. Execute. Create momentum. Don't stop.

Exercise agency, and be the person you're destined to be. Control what you can control. Don't let the rest kidnap your serenity. Be the best dentist, lover, spouse, friend, or child you can be. Naval Ravikant could have been talking to you about dental sleep when he wrote, "First you know it. Then, you understand it. Finally, you *are* it." Continue learning. Communicate effectively. Be kind. G.O. D.E.E.P. Transforming dental sleep begins with you.

SHOUT OUTS & ACKNOWLEDGEMENTS

There are so many people for whom I am thankful. It is impossible to name them all, but I'll try. Whether you find this book to be insanely useful or insanely wasteful, it wouldn't exist without the inspiration, influence, and incitement of these people.

To my family and friends, without your patience, guidance, generosity, and grace, I am nothing:

My muse, truthsayer, best friend, and soulmate, Lesia Tierney. Your energy is all I need to get by. My mother and father, Chris and Terry Tierney. Grandma and Grandpa Tierney. Bink. Aunt Janet, Uncle Chrissy, Uncle Matt, Uncle Dave, and the entire Tierney clan. Grandma and Grandpa Gregory. The Almighty Uncle Donnie, Aunt Debbie, Uncles Bobby and Jerry. Pagan Baby, Aunt Kathy and Uncle Lenny. Pidge – I wish you were here. Chris Kenyon – I miss you, David Joe Wyatt (RIP). Breyson Brawford aka Greyson Crawford. Larry Zenk. John Massie. Jeremy and Marlo. Tom Dyer. Matt Hodel. John "Junior" Randall. Alcoholics Anonymous.

To everyone that directly contributed their time, expertise, and experience to these pages:

Len Liptak, Kent Smith, Barry Glassman, Jason Doucette, Randy Curran, Steve Carstensen, Stacey Layman, Jagdeep Bijwadia, Scott Craig, Angela Kowaleski, Jeff Rodgers, Lesia Tierney, Matt Hodel, Max Kerr, Erin Elliott, and David Bolick.

Each of you added to my personal and professional life to make it rich and nutso:

Elias Kalantzis, Joel Blixt, Rani ben David, Mike Mohrhard, Brandie Havell, Mark Murphy, Stacy Ochoa, Jim Boyd, Sam Cress, Scott Jacobson, Kelley Nelson, Yoann Ojeda, Heather Whalen, Jamison Spencer, Greg Vogel, Jerry Vogel, Charles Collins, Ryan Javanbakht, Joey Yaller, John Bouzis, The Hill family, Kyle Curran, GoTo Sleep Center for CPAP Alternatives, Flora Teague, Michel Cowen, Brian Roasch, Joe and Don Frantz, Chad Wooters, Michael DiDomenico and Sleep Lab Magazine, Cindy Acevedo, Zeej Johnston, Barry Johnston, Madan Kandula, Rose and Jon BurtReynolds Nierman, Randy Clare, Suzanne Mericle, John Nadeau, Spencer Storbeck, Sunita Merriman, Saba Khalil, Revel and Waffles, Franz Wisner and Tracy Middendorf, Ragtime Tattoo, Tim and Iris Boyle, Quaka, Alex and the Dynaflex team, Terror Tacos, the Almighty TD$ Crew, Keith Thornton, Marc Newman, Gy Yatros, Andy Meek, Glidewell Dental Lab, Sonnie Bocala and Apex Dental Sleep, Chey Miller, Lisa Fischer-Herdt, Jim Szegedi, Don Malizia, Justin Elikofer, Daron K. Roberts, Joe Ojile, Avi Weisfogel, Sleep Review Magazine, Samantha T, Jason Anthony and Golden Rule Tattoo, Patty and Ken Berley, Amanda Culver, Matt Allard and Brandon Hedgecock, Matt and James at Lamp Pizzeria, Sleeping Around – The Podcast, Teresa DeNike, Carrie Magnuson, John Remmers, Somnomed, Kim and Beatrice at Panthera, Jim Swartout, Skip at MW, John Tucker, Vick Tipnes, Blackstone Medical Services, Norah Francoise Farouq, Dave Nothstine, Barry Johnston, John Viviano, Nick Layman, Jeffrey Rein, Joe Hoffman, Jaws 99, Neal Seltzer, Tiger and Olga, and Glax The Rippa, Bill Scheier, Steve Lamberg, James Cannon, Matt and James at Lamp Pizzeria, Oscar & Lupe & Freddie & the entire team at JJ's Deli. Colleen and the Dental Prosthetic Services team. Jonathan at FAY's Barber Shop. Steven Bender. And all the people I sit with in the back of the room cracking jokes.

To the authors, artists, athletes, and thinkers that soundtracked this effort and pushed me onward:

Toby Morse and H₂O, Hellah Sidibe, Rich Roll, Malcolm X, David Sedaris, Ryan Holiday, Anne Lamott, Tim Grover, Steven Pressfield, Daniel Pink, Eliud Kipchoge, Madball, Ice-T, Run the Jewels, Billy Joel, Rise Against, Oddisee, Foo Fighters, Tobe Nwigwe, Bun B, Mobb Deep, Ill Bill, Donald Miller, Youth of Today and Shelter, Gorilla Biscuits, MC Eiht, Confide, Inanition, Most Precious Blood, Killer Mike, Lil Dicky, Jason Fried and David Heinemeier Hansson, Strife, Sebastian Junger, Adam Grant, Naval Ravikant, Indecision, E-Town Concrete, Frank McCourt, lonelyboy, Seth Godin, Sam Harris, Malcolm Gladwell, Warzone, 88 Fingers Louie, VonDreaux, JB, Motley Crue, Jonah Berger, 12 Summers Old, Shane Parrish, Carl Fredman, Clipse, Mark Twain, Bane, Ludovico Einaudi, Montana of 300, End It, Cal Newport, Drain, BoySestFire, Shockwave, Ernest Shackleton, Bridge City Sinners, Die Antwoord, STIC.MAN, Perfect World, Froggy Fresh, Moby, Anacrusis, 7 Seconds, Bruce Springsteen, Spiritworld, The Business, Junior Smalls and the Criminals, Nas, DJ Muggs, Robert Greene, Kinghorse, Cross My Heart Hope to Die, Dead Kennedys, Christopher Hitchens, Kill Your Idols, Vybarr Cregan-Reid, Mindforce, Paul Kalanithi, Saltillo, With Honor, Dag Nasty, Bizzy Bone, Suicidal Tendencies, David Goggins, Sheer Terror, Yuppicide, Everlast, Habak, Doechii, Vision of Disorder, SSD, Arthur C. Brooks, Descendents, WU-Tang Clan, D.O.C., The Cure, Fear Factory, Slayer, Corrosion of Conformity, Balega Socks, Black Breath, Frank Turner, Harm Wulf, Zeal & Ardor, Danny McBride, City Morgue, Tommy Corrigan, Silent Majority, Blood Red, Capital, Leeway, Rodrigo y Gabriela, Deafheaven, Vanguard, DMX, Off With Their Heads, Devin the Dude, Brodnax, Jeff Gunnells and Cold As Life, King Fantastic, Slaine, Mogwai, Crank Lucas, Exhorder, CeeLo Green, The Casting Out, Scarface and Willie D of the Geto Boys, The Terrorists, Ganksta Nip, Minor Threat, Eamon, Del the Funkee Homosapien, Jay Electronica, Kool G Rap, Rick Rubin, Action Bronson, Mike Posner, Kevin Gates, E-40, Massimo Pigliucci, Defeater, Ignite, Lovage, David Banner, D.R.I., Blood For Blood, and Bill Withers.

Do you want to transform dental sleep with Jason Tierney or stay up to speed with his speaking appearances, eating contests, The FYL podcast, or other hijinx?

Visit www.JasonTierney.net to sign up for his newsletter and stay in the loop.

It's free, but it's worth at least twice that price!

p.s. Online reviews can make or break a book.

Show your support for Jason Tierney and help other individuals discover his books.

Simply find this book on Amazon, scroll to the review section, and click "Write a Customer Review".

Thank you for your purchase and reviews,

we appreciate it.

Made in United States
Troutdale, OR
10/26/2023

14009269R00159